WOLFGANG U. DRESSLER – BASILIO CALDERONE –
SABINE SOMMER-LOLEI – KATHARINA KORECKY-KRÖLL (EDS.)

EXPERIMENTAL, ACQUISITIONAL AND CORPUS LINGUISTIC APPROACHES TO THE STUDY OF MORPHONOTACTICS

ÖSTERREICHISCHE AKADEMIE DER WISSENSCHAFTEN
PHILOSOPHISCH-HISTORISCHE KLASSE
SITZUNGSBERICHTE, 915. BAND

VERÖFFENTLICHUNGEN ZUR LINGUISTIK
UND KOMMUNIKATIONSFORSCHUNG

BAND 32

HERAUSGEGEBEN VON
WOLFGANG U. DRESSLER

Experimental, Acquisitional and Corpus linguistic Approaches to the Study of Morphonotactics

edited by

Wolfgang U. Dressler
Basilio Calderone
Sabine Sommer-Lolei
Katharina Korecky-Kröll

Accepted by the publication committee of the Division of Humanities
and Social Sciences of the Austrian Academy of Sciences:

Printed with the support of the
Austrian Science Fund (FWF): PUB 862-Z

This publication was subject to international and anonymous peer review.
Peer review is an essential part of the Austrian Academy of Sciences Press evaluation
process. Before any book can be accepted for publication, it is assessed by international
specialists and ultimately must be approved by the Austrian Academy of Sciences
Publication Committee.

The paper used in this publication is DIN EN ISO 9706 certified and meets
the requirements for permanent archiving of written cultural property.

ISBN 978-3-7001-8714-1

Layout: Andrea Sulzgruber, Vienna
Print: Prime Rate, Budapest
https://epub.oeaw.ac.at/8714-1
https://verlag.oeaw.ac.at
Made in Europe

TABLE OF CONTENTS

INTRODUCTION 7
Basilio Calderone, Wolfgang U. Dressler

I. German phonotactic vs. morphonotactic obstruent clusters: a corpus linguistic analysis 15
Wolfgang U. Dressler, Alona Kononenko-Szoszkiewicz

II. Morphonotactics in speech production 53
Hannah Leykum, Sylvia Moosmüller

III. The acquisition and processing of (mor)phonotactic consonant clusters in German 77
Sabine Sommer-Lolei, Katharina Korecky-Kröll, Markus Christiner, Wolfgang U. Dressler

IV. Exploring phonotactic and morphonotactic constraints in the acquisition of consonant clusters in L1 French 101
Barbara Köpke, Olivier Nocaudie, Hélène Giraudo

V. The natural perceptual salience of affixes is not incompatible with a central view of morphological processing 123
Hélène Giraudo, Karla Orihuela, Basilio Calderone, Barbara Köpke

SUBJECT INDEX 138

Introduction

Basilio Calderone[1]
Wolfgang U. Dressler[2]

Language sounds are realized in several different ways. Every language exploits no more than a subset of the sounds that the vocal tract can produce, as well as a reduced number of their possible combinations. The restrictions and the phonemic combinations allowed in the language define a branch of phonology called phonotactics.

Phonotactics refers to the sequential arrangement of phonemic segments in morphemes, syllables, and words (Harris 1955) and underlies a wide range of phonological issues, from acceptability judgments (pseudowords like legal <blick> vs. illegal <bnik> in English or legal <*Pfraus*> vs. illegal <*Xraus*> in German) to syllable processes (the syllabic structure in a given language is based on phonotactic permissions in that language) and the nature and length of possible consonant clusters (which may be seen as intrinsically marked structures with respect to the preferred CV template). This volume deals only with consonant clusters.

The study of phonotactics entails a set of problematic aspects due to its nature. In fact, if, on the one hand, phonotactics is part of the phonological grammar of the language and appears as a rules-based system, on the other, it is controlled by a number of non-categorical, probabilistic and gradient constraints. Often the researcher is faced with a series of apparent contradictions and empirical problems that require critical comparisons of alternative explanatory models and, most often, an investigation of the 'interfaces' and 'intersections' between phonotactics and other levels of linguistic organization, particularly phonetics or, instead, only phonology and morphology.

However, this volume focuses on experimental, acquisitional and corpus linguistic aspects of *morphonotactics*, which represents an intersection area between phonotactics and the morphemic structure of the language.

In particular, morphonotactics deals with the interplay between the ordering restrictions of morphemes (the so-called *morphotactics*) and the

[1] CNRS, CLLE-ERSS, University of Toulouse (UT2), Toulouse, France.
[2] Austrian Centre for Digital Humanities and Cultural Heritage (ACDH-CH) of the Austrian Academy of Sciences, Vienna & University of Vienna.

phonemic sequences of consonant clusters (*phonotactics*). More specifically, a consonant cluster is *phonotactic* in the strict sense when it occurs within a morpheme (such as /kt/ in German *nackt* 'naked' or *Akt* 'act', or in English <act> or <detect>, or as /nd/ in German *Kind* 'child' or *Rand* 'edge', or in English <kind> or <sound>). A consonant cluster counts as morphonotactic when it results from a morphological operation such as concatenation (such as /kt/ in German *zuck-te* 'jerked', *tank-te* 'refuelled', and in English <kick-ed>, <thank-ed>). It is important to note that apart from clusters that are purely phonotactic (such as final /mp/ in English <limp>, or final /mpf/ as in German *Dampf* 'steam') or purely morphonotactic (such as final /md/ in English <seem-ed>; or final /ŋkst/ in German *lenk-st* (steer-2SG) 'you steer'), many clusters can occur both phonotactically and morphonotactically (e.g. the cluster /kt/ in German as in *Akt* 'act' vs. *zuck-te* 'jerked', or /nd/ in English as in <kind> vs. <sign-ed>). A much less frequent interaction between phonotactics and morphotactics takes place when phonological deletion produces a consonant cluster in inflection or word formation (as in German *Risiko* 'risk', *Risk-en* (risk-PL) 'risks', *risk-ant* (risk-ADJ) 'risky').

A main focus of several of the articles collected in this volume is the Strong Morphonotactic Hypothesis (SMH), as proposed by Dressler and Dziubalska-Kołaczyk (2006). The SMH claims that morphonotactic consonant clusters are favoured in processing and acquisition compared to phonotactic clusters. This implies a synergy of morphology and phonology, with the acquisitionist effect that morphonotactic consonant clusters are acquired earlier than corresponding phonotactic clusters. This was first interpreted as an earlier emergence of morphonotactic clusters (i.e. when a consonant cluster is first produced correctly), but Kelić and Dressler (2019) have shown for Croatian that it rather holds for mastery of consonant clusters (i.e. when a cluster continues to be produced correctly). As to processing, the SMH claims that morphonotactic clusters are processed more accurately and rapidly than corresponding phonotactic clusters. These claims have been restricted to languages or morphological components with a rich morphology, such as inflection in Slavic languages, whereas they may not hold for languages and morphological components with less morphological wealth, such as inflection in Germanic languages. See, for more on this, the chapter by Sommer-Lolei et al. in this volume.

The articles represent the result of a joint French-Austrian interdisciplinary project with the title 'Human Behaviour and Machine Simulation in the Processing of (Mor)Phonotactics' funded by the ANR (Agence

Nationale de la Recherche, ANR-13-ISH2-0002) and the FWF Austrian Science Fund (Fonds zur Förderung der wissenschaftlichen Forschung, I-1394-G23). The main focus of investigation of the project was the study of the psycho-computational representation of (mor)phonotactics in French and German speakers from two angles simultaneously: *human behaviour* and *machine simulation*. Both of them cover a broad range of activities: from computational simulations (computational models appealing solely to distributional information for the linguistic data and processing the statistical regularities of representative corpora) to longitudinal studies of acquisition (in order to test whether there are systematic differences with regard to the phases at which phonotactic and morphonotactic clusters are acquired), psycholinguistic analyses (aiming at verifying the psychological plausibility of hypotheses on the phonotactics/morphonotactics distinction) and production analysis (focusing on the phonetic repair mechanisms and the systematic differences in the production of morphonotactic and phonotactic clusters in actual speech data). The present volume contains five papers focusing on the acquisition, speech production, processing and corpus linguistic analysis of morphonotactic vs. phonotactic clusters.

The papers combine distributional analysis and experimental investigations based on large corpora or on the analysis of the speakers' behaviour in producing phonotactically marked structures such as consonant clusters.

The first paper of the collection 'German phonotactic vs. morphonotactic obstruent clusters: a corpus linguistic analysis' by **Wolfgang U. Dressler** and **Alona Kononenko-Szoszkiewicz** presents a corpus-based study of the obstruent clusters in German. In particular, the paper investigates the distribution, in terms of type and token frequency, of triple consonant clusters (excluding glides) containing two obstruents. The study is framed within the NAD (Net Auditory Distance) model, a net reflection of the difference between adjacent segments in terms of the manner and place of articulation (Dziubalska-Kołaczyk 2002). One main result discussed by the authors is that, according to NAD predictions, (at least triple) morphonotactic clusters are preferred over phonotactic clusters for German word-final position, which supports the Strong Morphonotactic Hypothesis (SMH, as described above). This must be compared with psycholinguistic evidence, as reported in the chapter by Sommer-Lolei et al. (below). The typological characterization of the German language with regard to the word-final and word-initial obstruent clusters, in contrast to Slavic and other Indo-European languages, is also discussed at the end of the paper.

The paper 'Morphonotactics in speech production' by **Hannah Leykum** and **Sylvia Moosmüller**† investigates the influence of morphology on the phonetic realization of utterances. The authors perform acoustic analyses of word-medial and word-final consonant clusters, which could occur both within a morpheme as well as across morpheme boundaries. The hypothesis underlying the study is that consonant clusters across word-internal morpheme boundaries (morphonotactic clusters) are expected to be more robust and more highlighted in speech production than consonant clusters within a morpheme (phonotactic clusters). The analyses are conducted in three different language types: a word language (Standard German German, SGG), a mixed-type language (Standard Austrian German, SAG) and a quantifying language (Standard French, FR). These three types were chosen to investigate whether language-type-specific timing characteristics have an influence on the highlighting/reduction of consonant clusters. Concerning the language type, the authors hypothesize that differences between phonotactic and morphonotactic clusters are more pronounced in SGG as compared to SAG, and the differences are expected to be greater than those in FR for both varieties of German. The results of the analyses fail to confirm the main hypothesis and reveal that there is no difference in respect of durational and intensity characteristics between clusters with and those without a morpheme boundary. However, as the authors state, the absence of any effects does not necessarily imply that no direct influence of morpheme boundaries on the realization of consonant clusters exists, thus overriding an impact on phonology. Besides language-specific timing characteristics, other language-specific differences could exist. The three investigated languages share a low morphological richness, raising the question of whether the morphological richness of a language determines whether phonotactic and morphonotactic clusters behave the same or not. It is possible that in morphologically richer languages, the information about the morpheme boundary is more important to ensure intelligibility.

The paper 'The acquisition and processing of (mor)phonotactic consonant clusters in German' by **Sabine Sommer-Lolei, Katharina Korecky-Kröll, Markus Christiner** and **Wolfgang U. Dressler** presents a set of psycholinguistic experiments testing the Strong Morphonotactic Hypothesis (SMH) which claims that morphonotactic consonant clusters foster processing and acquisition. The two psycholinguistic processing methods used are progressive demasking and lexical decision. The results partially confirm the SMH, showing a significant positive effect only for rich compounding, a partial trend for less rich derivational morphology and no effect for inflection, which is relatively poor in German and thus cannot facilitate lexical processing. A psycholinguistically important finding is that familiarity often has a greater facilitating effect than frequency. The acquisition part of the chapter presents longitudinal data up to 3 years (3;0) of age and quasi-longitudinal transversal data up to a mean age of 4;8. Since the data does not suffice for making separate statistical analyses for inflection, derivation and compounding, no facilitating effects have been found in previously reported analyses. This contrasts with the facilitation effects found in morphology-rich Lithuanian, Polish and Croatian inflectional and derivational morphology.

The paper 'Exploring phonotactic and morphonotactic constraints in the acquisition of consonant clusters in L1 French' by **Barbara Köpke, Olivier Nocaudie** and **Hélène Giraudo** focuses on the possible effects of age, position and phonotactic vs. morphonotactic status in the successful pronunciation of the different French consonant clusters. The authors analyse distributionally longitudinal CHILDES data from four children (aged 1;6 to 3;0) collected in spontaneous speech interactions between a parent and the child. The analysis shows a high variation of error types (such as reduction, substitution, omission, repetition, epenthesis, shifted cluster or mixed sounds) in the characterization of consonant clusters. A more detailed exploration of the individual developmental trajectories, however, demonstrates the presence of an overall developmental pattern with the number of omissions decreasing while the number of reductions increases within the age groups. Concerning the consonant cluster's position in the word, overall French children have a tendency to a left-side preference in the development of the pronunciation of clusters. Finally, also, the morphonotactic status of the cluster seems to have a significant effect on the development of pronunciation, although only in a medial position. According to the authors, this positive effect of the morphonotactic status should be pondered in relation to several factors inherent to the corpus which may modulate and affect the results. In particular, morphonotactic clusters are relatively scarce in French and they never appear in the word-initial position, in contrast to a medial position and especially the word-final position, which seems a less favourable position in early acquisition. This and other considerations led the authors to the conclusion that an extension of the study to later developmental stages in older children, with a consistent vocabulary between the age groups, is needed, in order to weigh in detail the influence of frequency and position effects in the error patterns related to the (mor)phonotactic status of consonant clusters.

The last paper 'The natural perceptual salience of affixes is not incompatible with a central view of morphological processing', by **Hélène Giraudo, Karla Orihuela, Basilio Calderone** and **Barbara Köpke** reports on a set of behavioural experiments testing the reactions of French adults in a letter search task. The authors discuss the issue of morphonotactic processing through the notion of morphological salience – the functional and perceptual relative prominence of the whole word and its morphological components – and its implications for theories and models of morphological processing. With regard to the SMH, the task was carried out using words that include the target letter after a morphonotactic boundary (e.g. *vivre* 'to live' which contains *viv-* as a morphological base (stem) and *re-* as a suffix, a marker of an infinitive) against those with a purely phonotactic one (e.g. *centre* 'centre' in which *-re* is not a suffix and *cent-* is not a stem). The main hypothesis is that morphonotactic segmentation should be facilitated due to a double salience conveyed in the boundaries, as it is not only phonological but also morphological. The effects of position, initial vs. final, are also explored. The final results show that prototypical morphonotactic sequences are processed faster than phonotactic sequences in a final position, suggesting that phonotactics helps to decompose words into morphemes by enhancing their morphological salience.

Taken together, the papers offer an interdisciplinary view of (mor)phonotactics, as they provide acoustic-phonetic, psycholinguistic and corpus-based evidence in support of the proposed theoretical claims about the nature of phonotactic and morphonotactic structures.

Another merit of the present volume is its crosslinguistic methodology, including two phonologically and morphologically relatively distant languages such as French and German.

Comparing phonotactically very different Germanic and Romance languages in the analysis provides a larger and more informative picture of (mor)phonotactics in these two languages.

Behavioural analyses are of particular relevance for the development of crosslinguistically valid generalizations on (mor)phonotactic processing. Psycholinguistic tests applied to the two languages may help to define a continuum of phonotactic and morphonotactic complexity, with respect to which the two languages will occupy partly different and partly overlapping positions. Similarly, the crosslinguistic differences which emerge from the analysis of speech production contribute to the definition of the continuum of (mor)phonotactic complexity.

We hope that this special issue will provide inspiring suggestions for further investigations, including interdisciplinary approaches, within the domain of the acquisitional, cognitive and physical aspects of sound organization in languages, thus contributing to our knowledge of how human speech structures are acquired, mentally organized and physically produced.

The volume is dedicated to the memory of our colleague Sylvia Moosmüller (1954–2018) who died shortly after finishing her part of the joint contribution with Hannah Leykum.

REFERENCES

Dressler, Wolfgang U. & Dziubalska-Kołaczyk, Katarzyna (2006) Proposing morphonotactics, *Italian Journal of Linguistics* 18, 249–266.

Dziubalska-Kołaczyk, Katarzyna (2002) *Beats-and-Binding Phonology*. Frankfurt: Lang.

Harris, Zellig S. (1955) From phoneme to morpheme, *Language* 31(2), 90–222.

Kelić, Maja & Dressler, Wolfgang U. (2019) The development of morphonotactic and phonotactic word-initial consonant clusters in croatian first-language acquisition, *Suvremena Lingvistika* 45(2), 179–200.

I. German phonotactic vs. morphonotactic obstruent clusters: a corpus linguistic analysis

Wolfgang U. Dressler[1,2]
Alona Kononenko-Szoszkiewicz[1]

1. INTRODUCTION

1.1. Aims

In this contribution we provide for the first time a typological characterology (in the sense of Mathesius 1928; Lang & Zifonun 1996) of the morphonotactics vs. phonotactics of a single language, compared to contrastive studies such as Dressler et al. (2015) on German vs. Slovak and Zydorowicz et al. (2016) on Polish vs. English. We focus on word-initial and word-final positions (cf. section 4) and on triple consonant clusters (excluding glides) containing two obstruents, because these are more typical for German than for many other languages. We approach them in terms of an interaction between Natural Phonology and Natural Morphology and the Beats-and-Binding phonotactics of Dziubalska-Kołaczyk (2009). We limit our investigation to standard vocabulary and exclude onomastics, because it contains clusters that do not occur in standard vocabulary, such as *gm-* in many place names (*Gmünd, Gmunden* etc.).

With regard to phonological typology, German, like other Germanic languages, is a rather consonantal language in respect of the relative amount of its consonantal inventory and its variety and complexity of consonant clusters (cf. Maddieson 2006, 2013; Donohue et al. 2013), although – in contrast to several Slavic languages, for example – German has syllabic sonorants only in an unstressed position in casual speech. German has several voiceless affricates, among the typologically rather rare ones the labial-labiodental /p͡f/ (Luschützky 1992). German is richer in consonant clusters word-finally than word-initially, in contrast to most Romance and many other non-Germanic Indo-European languages. Phonological typology, though discussed at least since Trubetzkoy (1939),

---

[1] Austrian Centre for Digital Humanities and Cultural Heritage (ACDH-CH) of the Austrian Academy of Sciences, Vienna.
[2] University of Vienna.

has focused on the characteristics of phonemes, phoneme oppositions and phoneme inventories. If phonotactics has been treated at all, then it is in terms of syllable structures. Even the recent publications of Hyman (2007), Blevins (2007) and Hyman and Plank (2018) mention consonant clusters at most in passing and never discuss triple or quadruple clusters (for contrastive studies of German, see section 1.6). This lacuna may be due to phonological typologists not working with large electronic corpora, which we do for German in this contribution.

In continuation of previous theoretical and contrastive work (Dressler & Dziubalska-Kołaczyk 2006; Dressler, Dziubalska-Kołaczyk & Pestal 2010; Korecky-Kröll et al. 2014) we are going to characterize German patterns of consonantal morphonotactics vs. phonotactics from a phonological, morphological, typological and corpus linguistic perspective.

We investigate prototypical rather than non-prototypical cases of morphonotactics, i.e. the prototypical case of merely concatenative shapes of morpheme combinations, particularly when they differ from the phonotactics of lexical roots and morphemes and thus signal morpheme boundaries, as in English *seem-ed* /si:m-d/ (i.e. there is no lexical final [-md] cluster in English). The non-prototypical case of morphological combinations resulting in vowel deletion is marginal in German, e.g. in *Risiko* 'risk', adj. *risk-ant* 'risky' (in contrast to the regular case of schwa deletion, more in section 4).

1.2. Phonotactics vs. morphonotactics

Morphonotactic clusters differ from phonotactic ones through the interaction of morphotactics with phonotactics (Dressler & Dziubalska-Kołaczyk 2006; Calderone, Celata & Laks 2014; Zydorowicz et al. 2016). More specifically, morphonotactic clusters are either due to the addition of a further morpheme, an affix in the case of derivational morphology or another lexical morpheme in the case of compounding, or due to a subtractive morphotactic operation which leads to vowel deletion, as in Ger. *silbr-ig* 'silvery' from *Silber* 'silver' (more in section 4.2).

Because of this interaction between morphology and phonology, it has been claimed (Dressler & Dziubalska-Kołaczyk 2006: 19–20) that in general morphonotactic clusters are less preferred than phonotactic ones. This contrasts with the Strong Morphonotactic Hypothesis (Dressler & Dziubalska-Kołaczyk 2006; Dressler et al. 2010), which states that in processing and first language acquisition the interaction of morphology with phonotactics facilitates both processing and acquisition. A further claim on the interaction between morphology and phonology has been made by Shosted (2006), who has found a (statistically insignificant) trend of a positive correlation between complexity in the syllable structure and morphological complexity. It would be worth separating phonological and morphonotactic clusters, because only complex morphonotactics should correlate with morphological complexity.

In order to define the level of deviation of morphonotactic (i.e. morphologically and phonologically motivated) consonant clusters from purely phonotactic (i.e. merely phonologically motivated) ones in German, we have applied the gradual scale proposed by Dressler and Dziubalska-Kołaczyk (2006). These are clusters such as the following English ones:

1) Clusters which are always morphologically motivated, i.e. never occur in monomorphemic words (cf. Dressler 1985: 220 f.). To this group belongs a consonant cluster /-md/ which always occurs in past participles due to concatenation of a sonorant with the suffix, as in *seem-ed, claim-ed.* Other examples of this group are the word-final consonant clusters /-fs, -vz/ as in *laughs, loves, wife's, wives*, which occur only in plurals, third person singular present forms and in Saxon genitives.

2) Clusters, which are morphologically motivated as a strong default, i.e. which are paralleled by very few exceptions of a morphologically unmotivated nature. For instance, the cluster /ts/ in most cases occurs across word boundaries, as in *lets*, *meets,* but also in morphologically simple words as in *quartz*, *hertz*. Moreover, in English a strong default is present in a cluster /-ps/ as in *steps*, *keeps*, except the borrowings from Latin such as *apse*, *lapse*, and *glimpse*.

3) Clusters, which are morphologically motivated as a weak default, i.e. which are paralleled by more exceptions of a morphologically unmotivated nature. An example is the consonant cluster /-ks/, which is always morphonotactic in the third person singular verb endings and in plurals as in *speaks*, *oaks*, and a phonotactic cluster related to the spelling <x> as in *fox, mix.*

4) Clusters, whose minority is morphologically motivated, i.e. which are quite normal phonotactic clusters and may also have some morphological motivation. To this group belongs the cluster /-nd/ that occurs across morpheme boundaries in past-tense verbs or past participles as in *grinned, tanned*. Moreover, as a phonotactic cluster, it is present in a number of words such as *hand*, *land*, *around*.

5) Clusters which are only phonotactic, thus never divided by a morpheme boundary, such as /rf, sk/, as in *turf, ask.*

The theoretical background of our contribution is Natural Phonology and Morphology (cf. Dressler 1984; Dziubalska-Kołaczyk & Weckwerth 2002; Dziubalska-Kołaczyk 2009; Kilani-Schoch & Dressler 2005; Dressler & Kilani-Schoch 2016), as well as morphonology (Dressler 1985, 1996a,b), of which morphonotactics is a part (Dressler & Dziubalska-Kołaczyk 2006). This approach not only strives towards descriptive und explanatory adequacy but also towards guaranteeing, at least partially, the psychological reality of the linguistic constructs. This demands a psycholinguistic perspective (cf. Korecky-Kröll et al. 2014 and Sommer-Lolei et al. this volume). In usage-based linguistic and psycholinguistic approaches (Bybee 2001; Bauer 2001; Tomasello 2003), it is often claimed that token frequency is important only for the question of storage (which is not an issue here), whereas only type frequency and the discrepancy between high type frequency and low token frequency is relevant for the productivity and profitability of patterns (cf. Du & Zhang 2010; Berg 2014). Here we compare type and token frequencies, in order to evaluate these claims with fresh data.

1.3. Beats-and-Binding model of phonotactics

We investigate consonant clusters in the framework of the Beats-and-Binding phonotactic model established by Dziubalska-Kołaczyk (2002, 2009) which is embedded in Natural Linguistics (Dziubalska-Kołaczyk & Weckwerth 2002) and specifically in Natural Phonology. It is a syllable-less model, which explains the organization of consonant clusters in a language where beats constitute vowels (or the marked option of syllabic sonorants) and consonants are typically non-beats. A core of the Beats-and-Binding model is the Net Auditory Distance (NAD) Principle, which started as a modification of the Sonority Hierarchy principle (Whitney 1865; Sievers 1876; Jespersen 1904; Ohala 1990), called the Optimal Sonority Distance Principle (Dziubalska-Kołaczyk 2002: 82). The present NAD model offers the broadest existing possibility for defining degrees of intersegmental cohesion (Bertinetto et al. 2006) in terms of binding between the beat and adjacent non-beats and between adjacent non-beats, including the preferredness of a cluster.

NAD stands for the measure of auditory distances between neighbouring phonemes and allows construction of the hierarchy of preferences from the most to the least preferred cluster. A preference is understood as basically a universal preference which can be derived from more basic principles (Dressler 1999). A cluster is preferred if it satisfies a pattern of phonetic distances in terms of the place and manner of articulation plus the sonority between clusters specified by the universal preference relevant for their initial, medial or final position in the word (cf. Dziubalska-Kołaczyk 2009, 2014).

It is generally assumed that consonantal languages have more dispreferred consonant clusters than vocalic languages. In order to operationalize this assumption and to determine the status of consonant clusters in German, a software package, namely the Phonotactic Calculator developed by Dziubalska-Kołaczyk, Pietrala and Aperliński (2014) based on earlier work by Grzegorz Krynicki, can be applied. The default parameter values of the calculator include the manner of articulation (MOA), the place of articulation (POA), and a hierarchy of S/O (sonorant/obstruent) distinctions. Due to the Phonotactic Calculator's settings, the maximum number of consonant sequences to be analysed is bounded by triple clusters. Therefore, the current analysis of cluster preferredness in German is demonstrated based on triple consonant clusters.

Let us present the general predictions for a triple consonant cluster C1C2C3V, first for the word-initial position:

NAD (C1, C2) < NAD (C2, C3) ≥ NAD (C3, V)

It reads: "For word-initial triple clusters, the NAD between the third consonant and the second consonant should be greater than or equal to the NAD between this third consonant and the vowel, and greater than the NAD between the second and the first consonant" (Dziubalska-Kołaczyk 2014: 5, also for the following citations).

For the word-final position VC1C2C3 it states:

NAD (V, C1) ≤ NAD (C1, C2)>NAD (C2, C3)

The condition reads: "For word-final triple clusters, the NAD between the first consonant and the second consonant should be greater than or equal to the NAD between this first consonant and the beat, and greater than the NAD between the second and the third consonant."

The condition for medial triple clusters VC1C2C3V states:

VC1C2C3V NAD (V, C1) ≥ NAD (C1, C2) & NAD (C2, C3) < NAD (C3, V2)

It reads: "For word-medial triple clusters, the NAD between the first and the second consonant should be less than or equal to the NAD between the first consonant and the beat to which it is bound, whereas the NAD between the second and the third consonant should be less than between the third consonant and the beat to which it is bound."

The NAD product indicates a mean number of all the distances between the neighbouring phonemes in the cluster. It was introduced to the calculator in order to assign a preferability index which is "a number denoting a degree to which a given preference is observed" (Dziubalska-Kołaczyk 2019). The formula for word-initial consonant clusters is as follows:

NAD product = NAD C1C2 – NAD C2V

Thus, it allows the clusters to be ordered according to their degree of preferability values from the most preferred to the least.

1.4. Principles of Natural Morphology relevant for morphonotactics

Natural Morphology is a theory of preferences (Dressler 1999; Dressler & Kilani-Schoch 2016) divided into three subtheories. Of the first one, which accounts for universal preferences, the most relevant for morphonotactics are the parameters of iconicity (especially constructional diagrammaticity) and transparency. In connection with the subparameter of constructional diagrammaticity, German morphonotactic consonant clusters are nearly always due to affixation, which is the most iconic operation, whereas anti-iconic subtraction, as in *risk-ant* 'risky', derived from *Risiko* 'risk', is very rare (more in section 3). High transparency favours morphological decomposition, which is undertaken automatically in processing: also from this perspective, affixation facilitates decomposition more than word-internal modification and subtraction, and when a consonant cluster is only morphonotactic, the morpheme boundary is more salient, which facilitates decomposition or segmentation (cf. Korecky-Kröll et al. 2014). Also, high morphosemantic transparency facilitates decomposition, whereas opacity hinders it (Libben 1998; Gagné 2009: 264–268; Hongbo, Gagné & Spalding 2011; Dressler, Ketrez & Kilani-Schoch 2017). For example, the relationship between Ger. *Kun-st* 'art' and its verb base *könn-en* 'be able, can' is both morphotactically and morphosemantically obscure (cf. below and section 2.2).

Within the second subtheory, typological adequacy, German can be characterized as a weakly inflecting language, whose morphology is moderately rich (except in compounding). Thus, compounding may create more morphonotactic clusters than inflection or derivation. Unfortunately, we cannot investigate systematically word-internal clusters due to compounding because of our corpus; there is a lack of corpus linguistic tools for doing this semi-automatically. German is also a more suffixing than prefixing language. That inflectional prefixation cannot create consonantal clusters, corresponds to the type of suffixing language to which German belongs.

Within the third subtheory of system adequacy, the criterion of productivity (Bauer 2001; Dressler, Libben & Korecky-Kröll 2014) is very relevant: productive morphological rules, such as plural formation, inflection for person and past participle formation, are liable to be involved in many more morphonotactic consonant clusters than unproductive rules, such as deverbal action/result noun formation, such as in *Dien-st* 'service' and *Kun-st* (see above). The endpoint of non-productivity is reached in the case of fossil morphemes, such as the prefix in *Aber-glaube* 'superstition', where the base *Glaube* 'faith' is easy to detect. Still we can classify its internal triple consonant cluster /rgl/ as morphonotactic.

Although, from a semiotic point of view morphology is more important than phonology for morphonotactics (Dressler 1985, 1996a), diachronic change may transform morphonotactic clusters into phonotactic clusters, but not vice versa (cf. Dressler et al. 2019).

1.5. Database

The corpus linguistic research was based on the data extracted from the Austrian Media Corpus (AMC), which was developed at the Austrian Academy of Sciences (cf. Ransmayr, Mörth & Matej 2017). It is considered to be one of the largest corpus collections of the German language. It covers all printed resources from Austrian printed media for the last two decades, including the transcripts of Austrian television and broadcast news plus the news reports of the Austria Press Agency APA. This corpus contains about 40 million texts of various genres containing about 10 billion word tokens. It is linguistically annotated with morphosyntactic information and lemmatized. Due to its functionality, a list of all word types and word tokens containing the specific clusters in a given corpus can be selected along with the frequency of occurrence and part of speech. Clearly the numbers of types (inflectional word forms) given in the lists below refer to what is attested in the AMC; the number of potential correct forms is higher.

The starting point of the research was obtaining the data from the AMC. The corpus automatically allows identification of the position of a cluster, thus different queries were specified in the research. For instance, for the word-initial position the following query was involved "str.+". It reads word-initial triple cluster /str-/ followed by one or more character. Thus, all consonant clusters along with their frequency of occurrence in the corpus were retrieved, according to their position in the word, for further analysis. The next stage included the elimination of all irrelevant words, such as proper names, misspellings or non-words. The last stage of the analysis was the division of the words into three groups depending on whether the cluster is only morphonotactic, only phonotactic or both.

The second analysis related to measuring auditory distances in the cluster via the NAD calculator, which was introduced in the previous section. All examples are written in the national German orthography. In the German consonantal system, a phoneme <ch> is a voiceless palatal or velar fricative; <sch> (and word-initial <s> before a stop) is a voiceless sibilant. For the NAD calculator /r/ is specified as an uvular liquid approximant.

All clusters will be presented according to their position and each cluster will be exemplified by a single word, selected according to its high token frequency. If the number of word types occurred fewer than five times in the corpus, these words were eliminated from the analysis because most of them consisted of orthographic mistakes or they were non-words (especially names).

1.6. German phonotactics

The phonotactics of German consonant clusters has been described several times. Meinhold and Stock (1980: 180–188) include in their description differences between positions and observe the influence of morphology and of phonostylistics. Hirsch-Wierzbicka (1971) aims to present an exhaustive overview of consonant clusters, but limited to monosyllables. Thus, several word-initial and word-final triple and quadruple consonant clusters are missing (to some extent also for monosyllabic words). There are also incorrect statements about disallowed peripheral clusters. A classical generative account can be found in Heidolph, Flämig and Motsch (1981: 977–990) with the concept of the phonological structure conditions of morphemes (formatives) vs. words.

Szczepaniak (2010: 107) and Fehringer (2011: 97) found specific, but very limited corpus-based evidence that German seems to avoid long word-final morphonotactic consonant groups, insofar as a rising number of consonants correlates with a rising preference for the masculine and neuter genitive allomorph *-es* instead of the allomorph *-s*. This presupposes a continuum for cluster complexity, whereas Wiese (1988, 1991, 2000; cf. Orzechowska & Wiese 2011, 2015) makes a sharp distinction between marked extrametrical consonants (the third and fourth most peripheral consonant of a cluster) and the other consonants of a cluster (more in sections 2.5 and 4.2); loan words are considered to have more extrasyllabic consonants, i.e. more complex consonant clusters (cf. also section 3).

2. WORD-FINAL POSITION

In contrast to most Slavic and Romance and more conservative Indo-European languages, Germanic languages are rather rich in word-final consonant clusters, of both a phonotactic and a morphonotactic nature. Moreover word-final clusters are more complex and more numerous and more varied in types than word-initial ones.

The morphonotactic clusters occur in the final position in 2nd SG. person and are mainly represented by 3rd SG. verb forms, superlatives or past participles, as shown in Dressler and Dziubalska-Kołaczyk (2006; cf. Dressler et al. 2010). They end with the suffixes *-st* (2nd SG., superlative, plus the unproductive deverbal noun-forming suffix) and *-t* (3rd SG., past participle and denominal circumfixes derived from the past participle, ordinal-number-forming suffix).

2.1. Quadruple clusters

All word-final quadruple clusters consist of a sonorant and 3 obstruents, the two last being always /st/. All are either only morphonotactic or morphonotactic by default.

The following 20 clusters are only morphonotactic (always 2nd SG., sometimes also 3rd SG. or past participle):

/-lkst/ (5): *melk-st* '(you) milk', ver-folg-st '(you) persecute',

/-rkst/ (30): *merk-st* '(you) notice', *borg-st* '(you) borrow', past participle *ver-kork-st* 'messed up'. The only phonotactic case occurs in the noun *Gwirkst* that exists only in Austrian dialects and means 'tricky affair': this does not count for the standard.

/-mpst/ (11): *pump-st* '(you) pump', *plumps-t* '(s/he) flops' = *plumps-st* '(you) flop' (with obligatory degemination of /s+s/),

/-mp͡fst/ (10): *kämpf-st* '(you) fight',

/-nʃst/ (3): *wünsch-st* '(you) wish',

/-nt͡ʃst/ (3): *plantsch-st* '(you) splash', recent English loan words *launch-st, lunch-st.* In oral speech, the /s/ is most often reduced after /ʃ, t͡ʃ / when followed by /t/.

/-lfst/ (3): *hilf-st* '(you) help',

/-rfst/(65): *darf-st* '(you) may', *nerv-st* '(you) enervate',

/-rmst/ (29): *form-st* '(you) form'.

/-lmst/ (8): *film-st* '(you) film',

/-lxst/ (2): *strolch-st* '(you) roam about',

/-rxst/ (11): *schnarch-st* '(you) snore',

/-ftsst/ (2): *seufz-st* '(you) sigh': normally the /s/ is fused with the preceding affricate,

/- xtsst (3): ächz-st '(you) groan' (same fusion),

/-rtsst/ (2): *stürz-st* '(you) fall' (same fusion),

/-lʃst/ (2): *fälsch-st* '(you) falsify', *feilsch-st* '(you) haggle',

/-ltsst/ (1): *salz-st* '(you) salt' (same fusion; 4 others potential, but not attested).

The following clusters are Gen.SG. of isolated masculine and neuter nouns:

/-ŋksts/ (1): *Hengst-s* 'stallion' (masc.),

/-rpsts/ (1): *Herbst-s* 'autumn' (masc.), plus its numerous compounds,

/-lpsts/ (1): *Selbst-s* 'the self' (neuter),

/-rnsts/ (1): *Ernst-s* 'earnestness' (masc.), plus its numerous compounds.

The four following quadruple clusters are morphonotactic only as a strong default:

/-ŋkst/ as in *denk-st* '(you) think' and in a variant pronunciation of *-ngst*, as in *sing-st* '(you) sing', superlatives *jüng-st* 'recently', the morphosemantically somewhat opaque adverb *läng-st* 'for a long time' (closely related to the transparent superlative *der/die/das läng-st-e* 'the longest'). However, there are two phonotactic exceptions: the nouns *Angst* 'fear' and *Hengst* 'stallion'.

/-rpst/ occurs as a morphonotactic cluster in 2nd SG. verb forms in *stirb-st* '(you) die', *wirb-st* '(you) advertise' (and their preterits). The only phonotactic exception is *Herbst* 'autumn' and compounds thereof (with diachronic loss of a schwa, cognate with Engl. harvest).

/-lpst/ is only morphonotactic in *stülp-st* '(you) turn up (the collar)' and *rülps-t* '(s)he burps' = 2nd SG., Part. *ge-rülps-t*. The transitional exception is *selb-st* 'oneself' with a fossil suffix, related to *der/die/das-selb-e* 'the same'.

/-rnst/ occurs as a morphonotactic cluster in 2nd SG. forms, as in *lern-st* '(you) learn', and as phonotactic only in the adj. *ernst* 'earnest' and its conversion into a noun.

Table 1 presents for each cluster the number of word types, its token frequency in the corpus and the type-token ratio. Since the NAD calculator is not able to measure all the distances within the quadruple clusters, no preferences can be deduced, but we chose the type-token ratio (TTR) calculation in order to arrive at some generalizations about the morphonotactic vs. phonotactic distribution of these clusters:

Table 1. Distribution of word-final quadruples

№	Cluster	Types	Tokens	TTR (%)
1	Vrpst	204	1,095,735	0.02
2	Vrfst	65	11,421	0.57
3	Vmpst	11	1,101	1
4	Vŋkst	37	9,688	0.38
5	Vrkst	30	5,149	11.38
6	Vrmst	29	255	10.38
7	Vrxst	11	106	1.29
8	Vmp͜fst	10	776	10.39
9	Vlmst	8	77	0.95
10	Vrnst	8	< 1,200,000	
11	Vlkst	5	526	0.82
12	Vnʃst	5	607	0.73
13	Vlpst	5	687	0.73
14	Vlfst	4	828	0.48
15	Vxt͜sst	3	3	100
16	Vlxst	2	2	100
17	Vlʃst	2	9	22.22
18	Vft͜sst	2	9	22.22
19	Vrt͜sst	2	4	50
20	Vnt͜ʃst	1	1	100
21	Vlt͜sst	1	1	100
22	Vŋkst͜s	1	23	4.35
23	Vrpst͜s	1	1,835	0.05
24	Vlpst͜s	1	25	4
25	Vrnst͜s	1	1,042	0.1

The type-token ratio is the most commonly used index of lexical diversity of a text, i.e. the number of tokens divided by the number of word types (McEnery & Hardie 2012), which allows us to analyse the lexical variation of vocabulary containing a specific cluster in the corpus.

It can be observed that: 1) the overall number of tokens increases along with the number of word types); 2) the growth of tokens is exponential. Thus, relying on the data from the AMC corpus, it can be concluded that for word-final quadruple clusters the number of occurrences is in direct relation to the type frequency. Although there are also some other exceptions, there is a group of clusters /-lkst, -nʃst, -lpst/ which consist of a sonorant followed by an obstruent plus /st/. They are relatively rare in types, nevertheless they have a high token frequency in the corpus.

Based on the TTR, the groups of word-final quadruple clusters can be clearly distinguished according to 3 intervals: 1) 14 with a TTR between 0.02 and 1.29%; 2) 3 with a TTR between 10.38 and 11.38%; 3) for 4 clusters the TTR is exactly 100%. In addition, there are 2 with a TTR of 22.22%, 1 at 4.35% and 1 with a TTR of 50%. The TTR in /-rpst/ is the lowest, which means that there are very few words of very high frequency, e.g. *Herbst* 'autumn' is the most frequent word with the final cluster /-rpst/ in the corpus, the frequency of occurrences being due to a great number of compounds ending in *Herbst*. The second group consists of /-rkst, -rmst, -mp͡fst/, again due to the fact that there are rather few words that occur frequently. Finally, the TTR reaches 100% in the third group, where two words have just one form and two others two forms in the corpus. All clusters which are morphonotactic only as a strong default are in the first, the largest group.

The highest type and token frequency of /-rpst/ is due to the richness and productivity of German compounding which leads to the high occurrence of morphonotactic clusters in compounds with the final element *Herbst* 'autumn'. Thus, the TTR is by far the lowest of all the quadruple clusters. The next lowest TTR occurs in /-nkst/ which is the only quadruple cluster that includes a phonotactic cluster, i.e. in *Hengst* 'stallion' and its numerous compounds. Something similar to compounding takes place in productive particle word formation. But this pattern generates final verb clusters only in secondary clauses such as *Wenn du den Schal um-häng-st* 'if you put the scarf around (your neck)', and therefore the token frequency of such word-final morphonotactic clusters is very restricted and thus cannot compete with the number of phonotactic clusters in compounds.

Thus, the type-token ratio proves to be a far better distinguisher of quantitatively similar groups than the type or token frequency.

2.2. Triple clusters ending in *-t*

As expected, triple obstruent clusters are more numerous and varied than quadruple clusters. Not all of them, but nearly all start with a sonorant. In addition to the two final obstruents /st/ we also find /ft/ and combinations of all existing obstruents with final /s/, of course excluding prefinal /s/ due to degemination of /s+s/ and prefinal /d, t/ because of the fusion of the dental stop and /s/ to an affricate /t͡s/. Due to such fusion, genitives ending in /ts/ also exist, such as des *Punkt-s* 'of the point'. We exclude from our investigation triple clusters consisting of 2 sonorants and 1 obstruent, such as /-lmt, -lnt, -rnt/.

The exclusively morphonotactic triple clusters are 24 in number, i.e. 13 more clusters than the morphonotactic quadruple clusters:

/-xst/: *lach-st* '(you) laugh', superlative *höch-st* 'most highly',

/-xtst/: 3rd SG. ächz-*t* 'groans' and its participles,

/-fst/: *schaff-st* '(you) create', adverb *zu-tief-st* 'deepest', *nerv-st* '(you) get on nerves',

/-mst/: *träum-st* '(you) dream', *bums-t* '(s/he/you) bump(s)' and its participle, *spar-sam-st* 'most thriftily',

/-ʃst/: *wisch-st* '(you) wipe',

/-pfst/: *klopf-st* '(you) knock',

/-tʃst/: *rutsch-st* '(you) slip',

/-ftst/: only in *seufz-t* '(s)he sighs' (and in the reduced 2nd person, see above, similarly in the following examples), and in the participle *ge-seufz-t*, and its derived verbs,

/-lft/: *hilf-t* 'helps', in weak past participles (e.g. *ge-golf-t* 'golfed'), and in *elf-t*, *zwölf-t* 'eleventh, twelfth',

/-lxt/: 3rd SG. and past participle *er-dolch-t* 'stabbed'

/- ltst/: *walz-t* '(s)he waltzes' and its participle,

/-ntst/: *tanz-t* '(s)he dances' and its participle, *ver-wanz-t* 'bug-infested', a circumfixation of *Wanze* 'bug',

/-lʃt/: only in *fälsch-t* '(s)he falsifies' and its participle and derived verbs,

/-mʃt/: only in *ramsch-t* '(s)he buys cheap junk' and its participle and derived verbs,

/-rtʃt/ only in *turtsch-t* 'taps (eggs)' and its participle,

/-nʃt/: *wünsch-t* '(s)he wishes' and its participle,

/-pʃt/: *grapsch-t* 'grabs' and its past participle,

/-rʃt/: *forsch-t* '(s)he researches' and its participle,

/-ntʃt/: *plantsch-t* '(s)he splashes' and its participle.

The following examples can never be the 2nd SG. (due to the phonological reduction of *-s*):

/-nxt/ in the only verb *tünch-t* 'whitewashes', its participles and its derivation into a particle verb,

/-lkt/: *melk-t* '(s)he milks', *folg-t* '(s)he follows' and their participles,

/-mpft/: *kämpf-t* '(s)he fights' and its participle,

/-mpt/: *pump-t* '(s)he pumps', *bomb-t* '(s)he bombs' and their participles,

/-rpt/: *zirp-t* '(s)he chirps' and its participle, *stirb-t* '(s)he dies'

/-lpt/: *tülp-t* '(s)he turns up' and *wölb-t* 'curves' and their participles.

There are just 2 clusters which are morphonotactic as a strong default (if we take 75% of types as the criterion):

/-lst/: *will-st* '(you) want', *puls-t* '(s)he pulses' (and 2nd SG.) and its participle, adv. *schnell-st* 'most rapidly', but clearly phonotactic in Wulst 'bulge' and its compounds. Doubtful are *Schwul(-)st* 'bombast' and *Ge-schwul(-)st* 'tumour', because most people can relate it to the base verb *schwell-en* 'swell'. But this relation may be classified as rather metalinguistic; there is as yet no evidence that it would be active in processing (e.g. priming) experiments.

/-rt͡st/ as in *schmerz-t* 'it hurts' (also 2nd SG. *schmerz-st*) and its participle, but a unique phonotactic instance in *Arzt* 'physician' and its many compounds.

The following clusters are ambiguous with either a morphonotactic or a phonotactic majority:

/-nst/ as in *dien-st* '(you) serve' and in the homophonous noun *Dien-st* 'service' with an unproductive deverbal nominalization suffix, *grins-t* '(s)he grins' (plus 2nd SG.) and its participle, adv. *fein-st* 'in the finest way'. The cluster is clearly phonotactic in *ernst* 'earnest', *sonst* 'otherwise', *Wanst* 'paunch'. We should also add earlier derivations such as *Kunst* 'art' which many relate metalinguistically, against furious artist's opposition, to the verb *könn-en* 'to be able'; *Gunst* 'favour', which few relate metalinguistically to the etymologically cognate verb *gönn-en* 'not begrudge smth to smbd'; similarly *Brunst* 'sexual heat' to *brenn-en* 'burn'. In terms of types (excluding compounds), the cluster /-nst/ might be called morphonotactic by default, but the 1,993 compounds with the second element *-kunst* render the global type and token frequency of phonotactic clusters the majority.

/-rst/ is morphonotactic in cases such as *war-st* '(you) were', the superlative adverb *schwer-st* 'heaviest', isolated *mors-t* '(s/he/you) send in Morse' and its participle vs. phonotactic *Wurst* 'sausage', *Forst* 'forest', *Durst* 'thirst', *erst* 'first' (which, like its English correspondent, was originally a superlative), but most types occur in compounds. *Ober(-)st* 'colonel' is thoroughly lexicalized (morphosemantically opaque), but clearly related to the superlative *der ober-ste* 'the highest'. When excluding compounds, the types are morphonotactic by default.

/-pst/ is morphonotactic in cases such as *tipp-st* '(you) type', *lieb-st* '(you) love', *pieps-t* '(s)he peeps' (also 2nd SG. and particple *ge-pieps-t*), superlative (or, more precisely, excessive) adverb *herz+aller-lieb-st* 'wholeheartedly dearest', phonotactic in *Papst* 'pope', *Obst* 'fruits', *Probst* 'provost'. Again, this cluster can be considered to be morphonotactic by default, when excluding compounds, but the abundant metaphoric compounds of *Papst* make the global type frequency and token frequency of phonotactic clusters majoritarian.

/-rkt/ occurs as a morphonotactic cluster in *merk-t* '(s)he notices' *sorg-t* '(s)he cares' and their participles, but as a phonotactic cluster in *Markt* 'market', *Infarkt* 'infarct' and their numerous compounds. Without these the cluster is morphonotactic by default.

/-ŋkt/ (written with also *-ngt)* is morphonotactic by default as in *bring-t* '(s)he brings', if one excludes the noun *Punkt* 'point, dot' with its numerous compounds, again as the richness of German compounding type and token frequency hides the basic default. Another noun with the phonotactic cluster is *Instinkt.*

/-rxt/ (phonetically [rçt]) is similarly morphonotactic by default, as in *ge-pferch-t* 'crammed', with the only phonotactic cluster in *Furcht* 'fear' and its numerous compounds.

/-rft/ is similarly morphonotactic by default, as in *wirf-t* 'throws' and *nerv-t* 'enervates', with the phonotactic exceptions *Werft* 'wharf' with its many compounds and *Notdurft* 'need' (where the earlier morpheme boundary before nominalizing *t* is obsolete).

/-nft/ is the only cluster of this subgroup which is phonotactic by default, as in *sanft* 'mild' (Austrian variant *Senft* 'mustard' with a secondarily attached final /t/). The only morphonotactic exception is the ordinal number *fünf-t* 'fifth', whereas it is improbable that an analogous morpheme boundary is processed in *Brunft* 'rut (of deer)', historically derived from *brenn-en* 'to burn', because of its morphotactic and morphosemantic opacity, and with most nouns analogously derived from particle verbs with the verbal base *komm-en* 'come', such as *Zukunft, Hinkunft* 'future' vs. *zukommen* 'approach, belong'.

/-kst/ (also written *-chst*, *-ckst*, *-gst, -xt*) is morphonotactic by default, as in *wächs-t* 'grows' (also in the 2nd singular *weck-st* '(s)he awakes'), the only phonotactic exceptions are *Text* 'text' and *Axt* 'axe' with their numerous compounds.

There are no other word-final triple consonant clusters with 2 final obstruents, unless in foreign names, such as *Minsk, Kursk*. Other comparable triple clusters with final *-t* do not occur, because conceivable and pronounceable clusters such as *-skt, -spt* do not occur as phonotactic clusters and, in contrast to English, they are excluded as morphonotactic clusters, because no verb roots (nor nouns) ending in *-sk, -sp* exist in German. Adjectives ending in *-sk* do not form a superlative in *-sk+st*, but insert an *-e-* before the superlative suffix. Other fricatives have a still smaller phonotactic distribution than /s/.

Thus, all word-final triple clusters, which contain two obstruents are morphonotactic (only exception: those in *-nft*), because phonotactic clusters either do not occur or only occur as the exceptions when counted in lemmas. But their type and token number may be competitive with morphonotactic ones due to compounding. Many of the lemmas with final phonotactic clusters go back to derivations with a morphonotactic cluster.

As expected, morphonotactic clusters ending in the longer suffix *-st* have fewer phonotactic counterparts than morphonotactic clusters ending in the shorter suffix *-t*.

Turning to a NAD analysis of triple final clusters ending in /t/, we start with the presentation of the frequency demonstrated in Table 2:

Table 2. Frequency ranks of word-final triples

№	Cluster	Types	Tokens	TTR (%)
1	ŋkt	6,196	9,831,812	0.063
2	nst	5,594	5,487,640	0.1
3	kst	2,136	2,457,398	0.09
4	nft	1,640	2,601,645	0.06
5	rst	1,401	5,649,995	0.02
6	rt͜st	1,226	1,399,699	0.09
7	pst	845	4,776,987	0.02
8	lst	360	92,894	0.4
9	rft	304	597,052	0.05
10	nt͜st	266	560,076	0.05
11	xst	246	1,838,731	0.01
12	mp͜ft	232	662,652	0.03
13	mst	226	164,703	0.14
14	lkt	182	2,809,304	0.01
15	rʃt	163	625,920	0.03
16	lt͜st	156	54,562	0.29
17	fst	136	89,308	0.15
18	rkt	134	1,358,674	0.01
19	rxt	104	87,843	0.12

20	mpt	98	157,983	0.06
21	rpt	90	294,409	0.03
22	lpt	50	11,632	0.43
23	lft	46	376,380	0.01
24	nʃt	45	354,583	0.01
25	ʃst	40	1,388	2.89
26	t͜ʃst	31	150	20.7
27	pʃt	27	5075	0.41
28	ft͜st	23	19,692	0.12
29	lʃt	22	52,109	0.04
30	xt͜st	19	9,353	0.2
31	nt͜ʃt	19	9,188	0.21
32	lxt	16	1,580	1.01
33	mʃt	10	770	1.3
34	nxt	5	2066	0.24
35	rt͜ʃt	4	4	100
36	p͜fst	16	374	4.28

In contrast to quadruple clusters, triple clusters do not form several neatly separated groups according to the TTR: the TTR of just 4 clusters is clearly above 1%, one amounts to 20.7% and only one has a TTR of 100%. None of the triple clusters hast just 1 type.

The NAD phonotactic calculator establishes the preferences of the clusters (structure VCCC) as presented in Table 3:

Table 3. Preference rankings of word-final triples according to NAD[3]

№	IPA transcription	NAD (VC)	NAD (C1C2)	NAD (C2C3)	NAD product	Preferred cluster?
1	Vrpt	2	6.6	1	5.1	Yes
2	Vrt͜st	2	5.1	0.5	3.85	Yes
3	Vrft	2	5.1	1.5	3.35	Yes
4	Vrst	2	4.6	1	3.1	Yes

[3] Three clusters /-nt͜ʃt/, /-t͜ʃst/ and /rt͜ʃt/ were excluded from the analysis because the NAD calculator does not recognize affricate /-t͜ʃ/. Therefore, they were counted manually.

5	Vlkt	2.5	4.8	1.3	2.9	Yes
6	Vlpt	2.5	4.5	1	2.75	Yes
7	Vrkt	2	4.3	1.3	2.65	Yes
8	Vrʃt	2	4.1	1.5	2.35	Yes
9	Vlxt	2.5	5.5	4	2.25	Yes
10	Vnkt	3	4.3	1.3	2.15	Yes
11	Vnxt	3	5	4	1.5	Yes
12	Vlt͜st	2.5	3	0.5	1.5	Yes
13	Vrxt	2	4.4	4	1.4	Yes
14	Vmʃt	3	3.5	1.5	1.25	Yes
15	Vmp͜ft	3	3	1	1	Yes
16	Vlft	2.5	3	1.5	1	Yes
17	Vmst	3	3	1	1	Yes
18	Vmpt	3	3	1	1	Yes
19	Vlʃt	2.5	3	1.5	1	Yes
20	Vxt͜st	5	3.5	0.5	0.75	No
21	Vnt͜st	3	2.5	0.5	0.75	No
22	Vlst	2.5	2.5	1	0.75	Yes
23	Vnft	3	2.5	1.5	0.25	No
24	Vnʃt	3	2.5	1.5	0.25	No
25	Vxst	5	3	1	0	No
26	Vnst	3	2	1	0	No
27	Vkst	6	2.3	1	-1.2	No
28	Vpʃt	6	2.5	1.5	-1.25	No
29	Vpst	6	2	1	-1.5	No
30	Vft͜st	5	1	0.5	-1.75	No
31	Vp͜fst	5.5	1	1	-2.25	No
32	Vfst	5	0.5	1	-2.5	No
33	Vʃst	5	0.5	1	-2.5	No

From Table 3 the following conclusions can be drawn:

The majority of preferred clusters start with a rhotic, lateral or nasal sonorant followed by two obstruents or another sonorant. The most significant distance between the neighbouring phonemes is always greatest when it starts with a rhotic or lateral sonorant, for instance the NAD product of /rpt/ is 5.1 and the NAD product of /rt͜st/ is 3.85.

Out of 33 word-final consonant clusters, 19 clusters are preferred and 14 dispreferred. If we add the 3 clusters that the NAD calculator could not handle, then we obtain 19 preferred clusters and 17 dispreferred clusters.

However, there is the question of whether similar predictions can be deduced in a simpler process of calculation. Since the NAD calculator is the most elaborate tool for deducing the predictions on the degrees of markedness for (mor)phonotactic clusters so far, it is worth trying to modify the method of NAD calculation.

Thus, we applied a factor analysis in order to test whether there is a correlation among the variables which were previously obtained in the present research. For the factor analysis, 30 word-final consonant clusters were selected and 7 independent variables. The first and second variables are the number of the word types and tokens from the AMC for each cluster followed by the auditory distances between the neighbouring phonemes according to the NAD calculator. The next two variables represent the information whether the cluster is preferred or dispreferred and the division between phonotactic vs. morphonotactic (Phon/morph) clusters as presented in Table 4.

Table 4. Factor analysis for word final triple consonant cluster

	Factor loadings (Varimax normalized) Extraction : Principal components (Marked loadings are > .700000)		
Variables	Factor (1)	Factor (2)	Factor (3)
Types	-0.024865	**-0.924373**	0.073853
Tokens	-0.142575	**-0.849302**	0.216074
NAD (VC)	**-0.832629**	-0.042204	0.403198
NAD (C1C2)	**0.916486**	-0.114682	-0.090996
NAD (C2C3)	0.051592	0.071495	**-0.966928**
Preferences	**0.918758**	0.024393	0.194894
Phon/morph	-0.283889	**0.730136**	0.201906
Expl. var	2.481534	2.129518	1.236691
Prop. of total. var	0.354505	0.304217	0.176670

Numbers in bold indicate a significant correlation among the variables. For instance, in Factor (1) we may observe a certain correlation between NAD (VC) and NAD (C1C2). The possible explanation is that if we look at the NAD table of all 30 clusters, we can see that the measures of NAD (VC) and (C1C2) are inversely proportional to each other in most of the cases. For instance, if the NAD (VC) is high then the NAD (C1C2) will be smaller. For example, in the word-final cluster Vfst the NAD (VC) is equal to 5 and the NAD (C1C2) is 0.5. And conversely, if we take the cluster Vrpt, where the NAD (C1C2) is equal to 6.6 and NAD (VC)=2.

The next observation is that cluster preferredness is related to the NAD (VC) and the NAD (C1C2). In general, if the NAD (C1C2) is higher than the NAD (VC), then the cluster is more likely to be preferred. This corresponds entirely to the NAD formula for triple finals shown above.

From Factor (2) we can see that there is a certain correlation between word types and tokens. They are connected in the same direction, so we could assume that if the number of word types grows, then the frequency grows as well.

For Factor (3) we can observe that the NAD (C2C3) is not connected to any of the variables, but it is still significant, presumably to other variables not yet discussed.

Most notably, the factor analysis has shown that the NAD (C2C3) is not related to the NAD (VC) or the NAD (C1C2), which goes against a well-established NAD formula for predicting the preferredness for word-final triple clusters. Therefore, one assumption that can be inferred is that the NAD distances of two phonemes in the cluster, namely the NAD (VC) and the NAD (C1C2) might be enough to decide on the preferredness of word-final clusters in German. However, more research on consonant clusters in different word positions as well as of different languages is needed in order to corroborate this statement. For that reason, we have compared the cluster preferredness of German, English and Polish in the word-initial and word-final positions via the NAD calculator when the most peripheral consonants were excluded from the analysis. The results are discussed in section 4.2.

If we compare the preference predictions in Table 3 or just compare its third and fourth columns, where the NAD (C1C2) should be bigger than the NAD (VC), and if we split Table 2 into two based on the frequency ranking, putting 18 clusters into the first half and 18 into the second, then we find 11 preferred and 7 dispreferred clusters within the first group, and 10 preferred and 8 dispreferred clusters in the second half. This is a positive, i.e. supportive, but not a significant difference. With regard to the claim that phonotactic clusters are more preferred than morphonotactic clusters, we found that among the exclusively morphonotactic clusters, 14 are preferred and 11 dispreferred, whereas among those clusters which are both morphonotactic and phonotactic, 7 are preferred and 4 dispreferred. This is again a positive but not a significant difference.

Moreover, all (but one) of the word-initial triple clusters, which are all exclusively phonotactic, are preferred clusters. And this seems to represent a very significant difference from the mainly morphonotactic word-final clusters. However, the triple final clusters ending in *-s* (discussed in the following section 2.3) are all exclusively morphonotactic and all preferred clusters.

2.3. Triple clusters ending in *-s*

A further source of word-final morphonotactic obstruent groups is the nominal -s Gen.SG., less commonly the homophonous plural suffix as in *Kalb-s* 'calf', (also plural), *Korb-s* 'basket', *Ge-zirp-s* 'chirping', *Schilf-s* 'reed', *Dorf-s* 'village', *Nerv-s* 'nerve', *Talg-s* 'tallow'. Parallel phonotactic clusters occur in *Rülps* 'belch' and *Mumps*. Similar morphonotactic clusters arise through the suffixation of plural *-s*, as in Gen.SG. and PL *Tank-s*, *Skalp-s* 'scalp', *Ulk-s* 'trick', and adverbial *-s,* as in *aller-ding-s* 'indeed'.

Word-final, exclusively morphonotactic, triple clusters with /s/ at the end are the following (all Gen.SG., if also plurals, then explicitly noted):

/-rps/: *Bewerb-s* 'competition', *Korb-s* 'basket' and their numerous compounds,

/-rfs/: *Dorf-s* 'village', *Wurf-s* 'throwing' and *Nerv-s* 'nerve' and their numerous compounds,

/-rks/ as in Gen.SG. *Bezirk-s* 'district', Gen.SG. and PL of recent English loan-words, such as *Park-s*. A phonotactic exception is *Murks* 'botch',

/-rxs/: *Monarch-s* with a few compounds,

/-rʃs : *Hirsch-s* 'stag',

/-lfs/: *Wolf-s* 'wolf',

/-lks/: *Erfolg-s* 'success', *Volk-s* 'people, folk',

/-lxs/: *Elch-s* 'elk' with several compounds,

/-nks/: also PL in the English loan word *Song-s*, only adverb *link-s* 'to the left,'

/-nʃs/: *Wunsch-s* 'wish' with a few compounds,

/-nxs/: only *Mönch-s* 'monk' with its many compounds.

/-nt͜ʃs/: only in English loan words, e.g. *Brunch-s* (more than 60% plurals, less than 40% Gen.SG. in the average),

/-mps/: only in English loan words (also PL), e.g. *Vamp-s*; a phonotactic exception is the loan word *Mumps*,

/-lps/ occurs only in *Kalb-s* 'calf' and in the loan word (also PL)

Skalp-s ‘scalp’ and their compounds; a phonotactic exception is the onomatopoeic *Rülps* ‘belch’,

/-mp͜fs/: *Kampf-s* ‘fight’ and its compounds,

/-mʃs/ only in *Ramsch-s* ‘junk’,

/-sks/ only in loan words (also PL), e.g. *Disk-s*.

The frequency ranking of these clusters is presented in Table 5:

Table 5. Frequency ranks of triple clusters ending in *-s*

№	Cluster	Types	Tokens	TTR
1	ŋks	10,218	5,608,107	0.18%
2	rks	4,398	858,787	0.51%
3	rfs	1,175	189,687	0.62%
4	rps	1,165	94,392	1.23%
5	lks	506	76,976	0.66%
6	lfs	56	13,961	0.4%
7	mp͜fs	20	35,000	0.56%
8	rxs	7	70,000	0.01%
9	rʃs	7	3,300	0.21%
10	lxs	6	268	2.24%
11	nt͜ʃs	5	370	1.35%
12	sks	5	145	3.45%
13	nʃs	2	176	1.14%
14	mʃs	1	6	16.7%

The spread of the TTR is similar to the triple clusters ending in /t/, but there is one cluster with only one type.

The preferences established by the NAD calculator for VCCC clusters are the following (see Table 6):

Table 6. Preference rankings of word-final triples ending on *-s* according to NAD

IPA transcription	NAD (VC)	NAD (C1C2)	NAD (C2C3)	NAD product	Preferred cluster?
Vrps	2	6.6	2	4.6	Yes
Vrfs	2	5.1	0.5	3.85	Yes
Vlks	2.5	4.8	2.3	2.4	Yes
Vlps	2.5	4.5	2	2.25	Yes

Vrks	2	4.3	2.3	2.15	Yes
Vlfs	2.5	3	0.5	1.5	Yes
Vŋks	3	3	2.3	0.35	Yes

Thus, all triple clusters ending in *-s* are preferred clusters, although all of them are exclusively morphonotactic, two of them with a marginal phonotactic exception.

Also, there are several morphonotactic double final morphonotactic consonant clusters with an affricate /ts/, due to Gen.SG. and rarely PL *-s*: /xts/ as in *Berichts* 'report', /kts/ as in *Projekts* 'project', /pts/ as in *Konzepts* 'concept', /lts/ as in *Anwalts* 'lawyer', /nts/ as in *Abends* 'in the evening', and /rts/ as in *Jahrhunderts* 'century'. The only phonotactic correspondents are words such as *Holz* 'wood', *Tanz* 'dance', *Scherz* 'joke', i.e. if a sonorant precedes an affricate.

A problem is represented by imperatives of the type *knicks*! 'curtsey!', *schubs*! 'push!'. First, it is unclear whether the word-final *-s* is synchronically still a derivational suffix. Second, even if not, it is unclear whether such imperatives are to be classified as base forms (if yes, then phonotactic) or as morphologically derived from the infinitive as a lexical entry.

2.4. Triple clusters ending in *-ts*

The masculine and neuter Gen.SG, *-s* (potentially, also of the homophonous plural suffix, but actually only in a single cluster) is the source of nearly always morphonotactic clusters ending in the affricate *-ts* due to fusion of the inflectional suffix with a stem-final dental stop (for frequency ranks see Table 7):

/-rsts/: *Durst-s* 'thirst',
/-lsts/: *Schwulst-s* 'bombast',
/-psts/: *Papst-s* 'pope', *Herbst-s* 'autumn' and their many compounds,
/-nsts/: *Dienst-s* 'service' and its many compounds,
/-rkts/: *Markt-s* 'market' and its many compounds,
/-nkts/: *Punkt-s* 'point' and its many compounds,
/-nfts/: *Senft-s* 'mustard',
/-rpts/ only in *Exzerpt-s* 'excerpt',
/-tsts/ only in *Arzt-s* 'physician' with its many compounds,
/-ksts/ only in *Text-s* and its compounds

Table 7. Frequency ranks of triple clusters ending in *-ts*

№	Cluster	Types	Tokens	TTR
1	rst͜s	8	2,434	0.33%
2	pst͜s	5	3,085	0.16%
3	lst͜s	5	389	1.29%
4	nst͜s	4	8,800	0.04%
5	rkt͜s	2	58,097	0.003%
6	nfs	2	301	0.66%
7	kst͜s	1	2,000	0.05%
8	rtst͜s	1	407	0.24%
9	rpt͜s	1	70	1.43%

Here we have no groupings of clusters according to TTR, but there are three clusters with just one type. Again, all clusters are preferred according to the NAD calculator, although all of them are exclusively morphonotactic.

2.5. Word-initial position

The German standard has no monoconsonantal prefixes, in contrast to Bavarian-Austrian dialects, as in *g'storben* 'died', *b'soffe*n 'drunk', *z'ruck* 'back(wards)' etc., corresponding to Standard German *ge-storb-en, be-soff-en, zu(-)rück.* Thus, the German standard is rather poor in word-initial clusters, all word-initial clusters are exclusively phonotactic. Some of the more dispreferred ones occur only in loan words from Ancient Greek and their derivations, e.g. /mn-/. German phonotactic initial double clusters were partially studied in Dziubalska-Kołaczyk (2002) with regard to universal phonotactic preferences. Moreover, double obstruent clusters serve as a basis for the complexity of triple initial clusters.

Phonotactic preferences for word-initial clusters in German have been studied by Orzechowska and Wiese (2011, 2015). They proposed an alternative approach to the NAD which is not limited to the size of the cluster and is not based on a sonority hierarchy but on an empirical analysis of features. The analysis of German initial clusters was based on 15 parameters, which included different values such as the cluster complexity, place of articulation, manner of articulation and voicing, in order to build a quantitative ranking of all clusters in terms of adherence to the preferences established by the Sonority Sequencing Generalization. This last approach will not be followed here.

For our study, the most interesting word-initial double clusters consist of two obstruents, particularly with a fricative in first position and a stop in second position: /ʃt-/ as in *statt* 'instead of' and /ʃp-/ as in *spielen* 'to play'. Words of foreign origin can also start with /sk-/ as in *skeptisch* 'sceptical', /sp-/ as in *Spatium* 'space', /st͡s-/as in *szenisch* 'scenic', isolated /xt-/ as in *chthonisch* 'chthonic', and /ft-/ as in *Phthisis* 'wastage'.

A fricative is followed by another fricative, or rather approximant, in /ʃv-/ as in *schwer* 'heavy', or in loan words in /sv-/ as in *Sweater*, /sf-/ as in *sphärisch* 'spherical', or /sx-/ as in *Schizophrenie* 'schizophrenia', and by an affricate in /t͡sv-/ as in *zwei* 'two'.

An obstruent is followed by a sonorant, first as a fricative, as in *schreiben* 'to write', /ʃm-/ as in *schmecken* 'to taste', /ʃn-/ as in *schneiden* 'to cut', /ʃl-/ as in schließen 'to close', /fl-/ as in *flach* 'flat', /fr-/ as in *fragen* 'to ask', /vr-/ as in *Wrack* 'wreck', only in loan words /sm-/ as in *Smaragd* 'emerald', /xr-/ only in the isolated learned loan word *Chrie* 'school theme', (/vl-/ only in foreign names such as *Vladimir, Wladiwostok*).

A stop is followed by a sonorant in /gr-/ as in *groß* 'large', /gl-/ as in *glücklich* 'happy', /gn-/ as in *gnadenlos* 'merciless', /kl-/ as in *Kleid* 'dress', /kr-/ *krank* 'sick', /kn-/ as in *Knie* 'knee', /bl-/ as in *bleiben* 'to stay', /br-/ as in *brechen* 'to break', /pl-/ as in *plump* 'clumsy', /pr-/ as in *Pracht* 'splendour', /dr-/ as in *drei* 'three', /tr-/ as in *tragen* 'to wear'. An affricate is the first obstruent in p͡fl as in *pflegen* 'to care for', /p͡fr-/ as in *pfropfen* 'to graft'.

A stop is followed by a fricative in words of foreign origin in /ks-/ as in *Xenophobie* 'xenophobia' or /ps-/ as in *psychisch* 'psychological'. A stop is followed by the fricative or approximant /v/ in /kv-/as in *Quelle* 'source', or by an affricate in /t͡sv-/ as in *Zwang* 'coercion'.

A sequence of word-initial stops is limited to words of Ancient Greek origin: /pt-/ as in *Pteridin* 'pteridine', /kt-/ as in *ktenoid* 'ctenoid'.

The majority of double clusters that do not occur only in learned words of foreign origin respect the preferences of the Beats-and-Binding-Model (Dziubalska-Kołaczyk 2002: 112).

In this contribution, we stick to the longer clusters with the maximum number of consonants in the onset, which is three. There are eight types of triple initial consonant clusters in German (see Table 8). All of them consist of two obstruents plus a sonorant or approximant: /ʃtr-/ as in *streng* 'strict', /ʃpr-/ as in *spricht* 's/he speaks', /ʃpl-/ as in *Splitter* 'splinter'; next in words of foreign origin /skr-/ as in *skrupellos* 'ruthless', /skl-/ as in *sklavisch*, adjective of 'slave'. In more recent loan words we find also / skv-/ as in *Squaw* (the only integrated loan word with this cluster, with the possible exception of *squash*), /spr-/ as in *Sprinter* and /spl-/ as in *Spleen*.

Table 8. Frequency ranks of triple word-initial clusters

№	Cluster	Types	Tokens	TTR (%)
1	ʃtr	15,371	2,451,048	0.63
2	ʃpr	6,317	2,861,933	0.22
3	skr	782	26,878	3
4	skl	221	3,175	7
5	ʃpl	104	6,131	1.7
6	spl	97	6,013	1.61
7	spr	25	15,420	0.16
8	skv	1	1,845	0.05

These triple clusters also exhibit no grouping according to TTR; only one cluster has just one type.

Table 9. Preference rankings of word-initial triples according to NAD

IPA transcription	NAD (C1C2)	NAD (C2C3)	NAD (CV)	NAD product	Preferred cluster?
sprV	2	6.6	2	4.60	Yes
ʃprV	2.5	6.6	2	4.35	Yes
ʃtrV	1.5	5.6	2	3.85	Yes
sklV	2.3	4.8	2.5	2.4	Yes
splV	2	4.5	2.5	2.25	Yes
skrV	2.3	4.3	2	2.15	Yes
ʃplV	2.5	4.5	2.5	2	Yes
skvV	2.3	2.8	5	-0.85	No

Table 9 presents the NAD analysis of these clusters and the quantification of rising preferences. For word-initial consonant clusters we undertook an analogous factor analysis as for the word-final consonant clusters in section 2.2. When eliminating the first consonant, the two remaining NAD distances, NAD (C2C3) and NAD (CV), again showed the same preferences as when including the first consonant, i.e. we arrived at the same result as in section 2.2.

In conclusion we can see that:

1) All word-initial triple clusters consist of initial double obstruent clusters of a s(h)ibilant plus a stop followed by a rhotic or lateral sonorant or the fricative/approximant /v/. Other double clusters which occur in the

word-initial position, i.e. /bl, br, gr, gl, gn, gm, dr, xr, xt, kn, p͡fl, p͡fr, ʃl ʃv, ʃr, ʃm, ʃn, ps, sf, sm, st͡s, t͡sw/ cannot be part of a word-initial triple cluster, except for extragrammatic words such as the interjection *pst*, which has the further irregularity of containing a syllabic fricative.

2) There is a moderate correlation between the degree of preferredness and the frequency in the AMC: the most preferred cluster is /ʃpr/, which has the highest token frequency and the second-highest type frequency; the next cluster in the hierarchy of preferences is /ʃtr/, which has the highest type frequency and the second-highest token frequency. The other three clusters differ little in preferredness and their frequency ranks decrease in parallel for types and tokens. The reason for the mismatch between the type and token frequency differences of /ʃtr/ and /ʃpr/ is on the one hand historical, insofar as they go back to the earlier clusters /str/ and /spr/, the only word-initial triple consonant clusters reconstructed with some certainty for Proto-Indo-European (Oppermann 2004). On the other hand, the general phonotactic preference for /ʃpr/ may have had a positive impact on its token frequency. The only dispreferred cluster /skv/ is rare and occurs only in one word type (or two).

3. WORD-INTERNAL POSITION

Word-internal clusters are presented only briefly and selectively for the following reasons: first of all, word-medial consonant clusters are much more varied and complex than initial and final ones, so that an equally extensive study would exceed space limits. Second, the corpus linguistic tools of the AMC do not permit the same procedures of analysis as for initial and final clusters. Third, the NAD calculator cannot predict preferences for the many complex clusters of more than three consonants. Fourth, internal clusters are psycholinguistically less important than peripheral clusters due to the bathtub effect, which renders the periphery of a unit better perceivable than its interior (Aitchison 2003: 138). Therefore, we limit our discussion to observations of general differences between morphonotactic and phonotactic consonant clusters and their explanations.

It holds for phonotactic clusters that word-internal syllable onsets always follow the pattern of word-initial onsets. In compounding and derivation, the syllable boundary always follows the morpheme boundary in consonant clusters.

In a word-internal position, there is a much greater variety of consonant clusters than in the peripheral positions. Phonotactic clusters that occur only word-internally have an internal syllable boundary, but they are rather few, such as /fk, dl, dv/ as in the plant name *Levkoje*, in *Adler* 'eagle', where a vowel has been lost, and *Advent* 'advent', where a morpheme boundary has been lost, and /tl/ as in the loan word *Atlas*. There are a few triconsonantal phonotactic clusters, such as /ktr, ltr, mpl, rt͡sn, stm, / as in the loan words *Spektrum, Altruismus* 'altruism', *Amplitude* 'amplitude', *Arznei* 'medicine', *Asthma*, thus hardly any with two obstruents.

The bulk of new word-internal consonant clusters are morphonotactic due to the addition of morpheme-initial to morpheme-final clusters in compounding and affixation. This often creates morphonotactic clusters which are disallowed word-initially or word-finally and may contain more consonants than are permitted in the word periphery. Examples are the compound *Herbst+pflanze* 'autumn plant' and the suffixation *herbst-lich* 'autumnal', as well as the prefixation *ent-springen* 'originate'. In compounding, interfixation may either break up (by the interfix *-e-*) or increase (by the much more frequent interfix *-s-*) the sequence of consonants as in *Weg+e+lagerer* 'highwayman' and *König+s+schloss* 'royal castle'. The syllable boundary is always after the interfix, which fits with the fact that the main morpheme boundary is always after, and never before, the interfix.

Verb prefixation and particle verb formation creates new word-internal consonant clusters as well. For example, the separable particle *ab-* motivates the exclusively morphonotactic clusters /p-d, p-t, p-g, p-k, p-ʃ, p-t͡s, p-v/, as in *ab-drehen* 'turn off', *ab-geben* 'give in', *ab-kommen* 'get away', *ab-treten* 'wear out', *ab-schaffen* 'abolish', *ab-wickeln* 'unwind', *ab-ziehen* 'remove', (with the addition of longer clusters, as in *ab-streiten* 'deny'). Moreover, some of the few non-separable verbal prefixes create new clusters, as with *ent-*, and the earlier but now only vestigial affix *ant-* as in *Ant-wort* 'answer'; in the parallel formation *Antlitz* 'face' the morpheme boundary was lost, and the cluster became a phonotactic one. A morpheme boundary must also be assumed after cranberry morphs, as in *Sint-flut* 'deluge', cf. *Flut* 'flood'.

In contrast to many non-Germanic Indo-European languages, German affixation does not provoke internal vowel deletion and internal morphonotactic clusters caused by it, other than of the weakest vowel schwa. An exception is *Risiko* 'risk' → adj. *risk-ant*. An epenthetic schwa is lost before a (originally word-final) sonorant in derivation, such as in the derived adjectives *adl-ig* 'noble', *silbr-ig* 'silvery' (more examples in Meinhold & Stock 1980: 197–201). Inflectional affixation results even more rarely in subtraction, which creates morphonotactic clusters, such as in *Risk-en*, the plural of *Risiko* (in contrast to the much greater frequency in Slavic languages, Latin, Greek and other ancient Indo-European languages).

In addition, word formation creates geminate consonants which are disallowed morpheme-internally, and phonotactically, with even more marked results; pseudogeminates are created by syllable- and morpheme-final obstruent devoicing, as in *ab-bauen* 'dismantle' with /p, b/.

Among clusters which are both phonotactic and morphonotactic, the productive word formation devices of compounding, verbal prefixation and particle verb formation may greatly outweigh the proportion of phonotactic clusters in types and tokens, e.g. for clusters starting with /-st-/, as in *west+römisch* 'Western Roman' and *aus-treiben* 'drive out' as opposed to phonotactic cases in loan words, such as *Pastrami*. This may create problems for matching phonotactic and morphonotactic clusters in psycholinguistic tests.

Only the complexity of consonant clusters, at least in terms of the number of member consonants and of the creation of new clusters which are not allowed in phonotactics, rises due to morphological operations. And in this sense, morphonotactic clusters are, on average, more marked than phonotactic clusters.

4. CONCLUSIONS

4.1. General results

The claim that in general morphonotactic clusters are more dispreferred than phonotactic clusters (Dressler & Dziubalska-Kołaczyk 2006: 83, Zydorowicz et al. 2016: 19–20) has been disproven for German peripheral triple consonant clusters. This removes an apparent contradiction between the claim and external psycholinguistic evidence from acquisition and processing experiments. In the first language acquisition of at least the richly inflecting languages Polish and Lithuanian, morphonotactic clusters are acquired earlier than phonotactic clusters (Zydorowicz 2010, Kamandulytė-Merfeldienė 2015). And at least in certain psycholinguistic experiments (cf. the other contributions to this volume), morphonotactic clusters are processed more quickly than phonotactic ones. Therefore, the claim that morphonotactic clusters are more dispreferred than phonotactic clusters should be dropped.

This conclusion is also supported by the ease of diachronic introduction of new, i.e. morphonotactic clusters into languages that lacked them.

A further finding on diachrony is that we have found in German, in analogy to what has been found in other languages, examples of the lexical development of morphonotactic clusters into phonotactic ones because of morphosemantic opacity leading to the loss of morpheme boundaries, as in *Brunst* 'ardour, lust' no longer being related to its former verb base *brenn-en* 'burn', except metalinguistically (cf. Dressler et al. 2019)

Similarly to many other languages, quadruple clusters can be reduced in casual speech. Thus, the normal pronunciation of 2nd SG. *wäsch-st* '(you) wash' is [vɛʃt]. These instances are fairly regular if the NAD distance is minimal, as in this case.

Probably, segmentally identical phonotactic and morphonotactic clusters have different vowel durations (cf. Plag 2014; Zimmerer, Scharinger & Reetz 2014), but it is, as yet, unclear whether these differences lie above the threshold of perceptibility. Moreover, other studies contradict these findings (see the discussion in Leykum & Moosmüller, this volume). In any event, Plag is right in objecting to linguistic models which crucially contain a flow-chart from one submodule to another in a way which presupposes bracket erasure (also criticized in Brown & Hippisley 2012: 273). Our model of morphonotactics (Dressler & Dziubalska-Kołaczyk 2006; Dressler et al. 2010; Korecky-Kröll et al. 2014) does not presuppose such bracket erasure. This also fits Slovak word-medial patterns: assuming that in a flow-chart, inflectional morphology follows derivational morphology, the derivational boundary in *potok* 'stream' must not be erased in order to prevent vowel deletion in Gen.SG. *po-tok-a/u*, in contrast to the deletion of the second vowel in the oblique cases of *ist-ok* 'source' and *otec* 'father' (Dressler et al. 2015).

For results regarding NAD calculations, see section 2.

4.2. Typological conclusions

Phonotactic asymmetries between word-initial, word-final and word-medial positions are well known. This starts with how the universal preference for CV structures (Dziubalska-Kołaczyk 2002, 2009) is realized in the three positions and depending on whether a word is monosyllabic, disyllabic or polysyllabic.

What is interesting for the typological characterization of German is the much greater variety and complexity of word-final than of word-initial clusters, e.g. in contrast to Slavic languages, Latin, Greek and other Indo-European languages. This asymmetry is also reflected in greater type and token frequencies for word-final than for word-initial obstruent clusters.

Type frequency asymmetries proved to be radicalized in token frequency differences, which means that the dominant patterns are more profitable.

This asymmetry has two sources: on the one hand, we have the diachronic result of prehistoric or early historic major vowel deletions in German word-final positions as opposed to the optimal preservation of vowels in word-initial positions. Those lost vowels of word-final syllables were all unstressed, which was not the case for word-initial syllables. On the other hand, we have the more important consequence of German having many short derivational and inflectional suffixes which are monoconsonantal or biconsonantal. But due to the restriction of morphological consonantism to very few consonants, already identified by Jakobson (1962: 108) for Indo-European languages, in German we find only final morphonotactic clusters ending in *-t, -s, -st, -ts*. Therefore, it seems a paradox that we find a still more radical restriction for final phonotactic clusters, namely to *-t, -st* and to nouns. The reason is again diachronic: all the final phonotactic nominal triple clusters go back or seem to go back to morphonotactic clusters with a final suffix now ending in *-t* due to the loss of unstressed vowels that followed them or a *-t* added secondarily in early New High German as a phonological addition, as in *Werft* 'shipyard', *Axt* 'axe', *Obst* 'fruit', *sonst* 'otherwise', dialectal *Senft* 'mustard' (Kluge & Götze 1957 sub vocibus).

Word-internally, the contrast between exclusively morphonotactic and exclusively phonotactic triconsonantal clusters seems to be even bigger. Also, here most triconsonantal clusters with two obstruents are only morphonotactic. An among ambiguous consonant clusters, the frequencies of morphonotactic clusters seem to be higher than those of phonotactic clusters. For efficient calculation of these frequency relations, new text-technological tools must be developed.

The fact that in German peripheral positions the NAD preferences for consonant clusters are identical irrespective of whether the most peripheral consonant is included or excluded in the NAD calculations, seems to be specific for Germanic languages. When we checked peripheral consonant clusters in Polish and English according to the list of clusters in Zydorowicz et al. (2016), we found that the (dis)preferredness of consonant clusters is different in Polish depending on whether the most peripheral consonants are included or excluded, but not in English.

Polish and at least Slovak among other Slavic languages (Dressler et al. 2015) differ from German and English with regard to peripheral triple consonant clusters in the following features, which appear to be relevant for the impact of the most peripheral consonant on cluster preferences when they are added to the more interior double consonant clusters:

First of all, the two Slavic languages are consonantal languages to a higher extent than the two Germanic languages. They have a much higher number of different triple consonant clusters than the two Germanic languages. For example, Polish has more than a hundred word-initial triple clusters, German only eight.

Second, Polish has many more word-initial triple morphonotactic clusters in tokens than phonotactic clusters; the two Germanic languages have no word-initial morphonotactic clusters.

Third, for word-final triple consonant clusters, the two Germanic languages have many more morphonotactic than phonotactic clusters, all of them due to the morphological operation of suffixation (i.e. addition). Polish and Slovak have only word-final morphonotactic clusters created through the subtractive morphological operation of deletion of the word-final stem vowel in the genitive plural, e.g. in Pol. *zemst* vs. Nom.SG. *zemsta* 'revenge', Slov. *pomst* vs. Nom.SG. *pomsta* 'revenge'. In addition, Polish and other Slavic languages also create word-initial and word-medial consonant clusters due to vowel deletion in inflection and derivation, as in Pol. Gen.SG. *ps-a* from *pies* 'dog'. German has only rare word-medial cases (see section 3).

Fourth, the most peripheral German consonants in triple consonant clusters in a word-initial position are only /s/ and /ʃ/ (in English only /s/), whereas Polish and Slovak also have many other consonants in this position. In word-final position the most peripheral consonants in German are only /t, s, t͜s/, in English /t, d, s, z/. These consonants are also the preferred final consonants in double clusters. By contrast, many different final consonants occur in Polish and Slovak word-final clusters. Thus, it seems that in the case of strong restrictions on the selection of the most peripheral consonants, the selection is natural, in the sense of not changing the (dis)preferredness of the interior consonant clusters to which they are added. This is reminiscent of those phonotactic analyses which assume for German, as for many other languages, that any third consonant in a tautosyllabic consonant cluster is extrasyllabic or extrametrical (see Wiese 1988, 2000).

This may also explain why, in the diachronic development of German, /t/ was sometimes added to a word-final consonant, as in *Axt* 'axe', *Palast* 'palace', *Obst* 'fruit' from MHG *obes*, *Sekt* 'sparkling wine' from Fr. *vin sec*, dialectal Austrian German *Senft* ← *Senf* 'mustard'.

4.3. Considerations on working with large electronic corpora

Working with large electronic corpora allows us to arrive at more reliable quantitative results. Here, the type-token ratio is very low for all triple clusters. For quadruple clusters we found (see section 2.1) distinct groupings within the whole range from 0.01% to 100%. Thus, the numerically most complex clusters behave differently than the less complex and more numerous triple clusters. The largest subgroup of quadruple clusters has a similar TTR distribution to the triple ones and contains the only four clusters which also include a small phonotactic minority. The more numerous groups of quadruple clusters are only morphonotactic: this again indicates the marked character of complex consonant clusters.

Our corpus-based study relied on the huge electronic corpus AMC, which may be the most complete print media corpus for any nation. This enhanced reliability for quantitative generalizations about the distribution of morphological and lexical patterns of consonant clusters. The disadvantage that such big corpora include many erroneous types of words was at least partially corrected for by manual exclusion of errors and by the restriction to types which have at least 5 tokens in the corpus. We included clusters with fewer than 5 tokens only if the cluster would otherwise not have been represented in our description. In discussions with other native speakers of German we could not think of any potential morphonotactic cluster which does not occur in the AMC.

Clearly new automatic tools should be developed for reducing the error-prone nature of large electronic corpora. More efficient tools are also needed for pattern searches, as we ascertained when studying word-internal clusters.

Even with better tools, the evidence from such an electronic corpus of written adult and adult-directed speech must be considered with caution. The AMC represents just one genre, and it has been found, at least for Modern Greek and Balto-Slavic languages (Dressler et al. 2017) that the distribution of lexical and morphological patterns may differ significantly for different genres.

REFERENCES

Aitchison, Jean (2003) *Words in the Mind: An Introduction to the Mental Lexicon.* 3rd Ed. Oxford: Wiley-Blackwell.

Bauer, Laurie (2001) *Morphological Productivity.* Cambridge: Cambridge University Press.

Berg, Thomas (2014) On the relationship between type and token frequency, *Journal of Quantitative Linguistics* 21(3), 199–222.

Bertinetto, Pier Marco; Scheuer, Sylwia; Dziubalska-Kołaczyk, Katarzyna & Agonigi, Maddalena (2006) Intersegmental cohesion and syllable division in Polish. Extended version. *Quaderni del Laboratorio di Linguistica* 6. Pisa: Scuola Normale Superiore.

Blevins, Juliette (2007) The importance of typology in explaining recurrent sound patterns, *Linguistic Typology* 11, 107–113.

Brown, Dunstan & Hippisley, Andrew (2012) Network Morphology. Cambridge: Cambridge University Press.

Bybee, Joan (2001) *Phonology and Language Use.* Cambridge: Cambridge University Press.

Calderone, Basilio; Celata, Chiara & Laks, Bernard (2014) Theoretical and empirical approaches to phonotactics and morphonotactics, Introduction to special volume on phonotactics and morphonotactics, *Language Sciences* 46, 1–5.

Donohue, Mark; Hetherington, Rebecca; McElvenny, James & Dawson, Virginia (2013) *World Phonotactics Database.* Canberra: Department of Linguistics, Australian National University.

Dressler, Wolfgang U. (1984) Explaining Natural Phonology. *Phonology Yearbook* 1, 29–51.

Dressler, Wolfgang U. (1985) *Morphonology: The Dynamics of Derivation.* Ann Arbor, Mich.: Karoma Publishers.

Dressler, Wolfgang U. (1996a) A functionalist semiotic model of morphonology. In: Singh, Rajendra (ed.) *Trubetzkoy's Orphan.* Amsterdam: Benjamins, 67–83.

Dressler, Wolfgang U. (1996b) Reply to Janda and Walker. In: Singh, Rajendra (ed.) *Trubetzkoy's Orphan.* Amsterdam: Benjamins, 102–105.

Dressler, Wolfgang U. (1999) On a semiotic theory of preferences in language. *Peirce Seminar Papers* 4, 389–415.

Dressler, Wolfgang U. & Dziubalska-Kołaczyk, Katarzyna (2006) Proposing morphonotactics, *Italian Journal of Linguistics* 18, 249–266.

Dressler, Wolfgang U.; Dziubalska-Kołaczyk, Katarzyna & Pestal, Lina (2010) Change and Variation in Morphonotactics, *Folia Linguistica Historica* 31, 51–67.

Dressler, Wolfgang U.; Hliničanová, Miroslava; Ďurčo, Matej; Mörth, Karlheinz & Korecky-Kröll, Katharina (2015) Phonotactic vs. morphonotactic obstruent clusters in Slovak and German, *Italian Journal of Linguistics* 27, 45–60.

Dressler, Wolfgang U.; Ketrez, F. Nihan & Kilani-Schoch, Marianne (eds) (2017) *Nominal Compound Acquisition.* Amsterdam: Benjamins.

Dressler, Wolfgang U. & Kilani-Schoch, Marianne (2016) Natural Morphology. In: Hippisley, Andrew & Stump, Gregory (eds) *The Cambridge Handbook of Morphology.* Cambridge: Cambridge University Press, 356–389. doi:10.1017/9781139814720.014

Dressler, Wolfgang U.; Kononenko, Alona; Sommer-Lolei, Sabine; Korecky-Kröll, Katharina; Zydorowicz, Paulina & Kamandulytė-Merfeldienė, Laura (2019) Morphological richness and transparency and the genesis and evolution of morphonotactic patterns, *Folia Linguistica Historica* 40(1), 85–106. doi:10.1515/flih-2019-0005

Dressler, Wolfgang U.; Libben, Gary & Korecky-Kröll, Katharina (2014) Conflicting vs. convergent vs. interdependent motivations in morphology. In: MacWhinney, Brian; Malchukov, Andrej & Moravcsik, Edith (eds) *Competing Motivations in Grammar and Usage*. Oxford: Oxford University Press, 181–196.

Du, Lifang & Zhang, Xuezhong (2010) A survey of the measurements of morphological productivity, *English Language Teaching* 3, 60–63.

Dziubalska-Kołaczyk, Katarzyna (2002) *Beats-and-Binding Phonology*. Frankfurt: Lang.

Dziubalska-Kołaczyk, Katarzyna (2009) NP extension: B&B phonotactics, *PSiCL* 45, 55–71.

Dziubalska-Kołaczyk, Katarzyna (2014) Explaining phonotactics using NAD, *Language Sciences* 46, 6–17.

Dziubalska-Kołaczyk, Katarzyna (2019) On the structure, survival and change of consonant clusters, *Folia Linguistica Historica* 53(s40-1), 107–127.

Dziubalska-Kołaczyk, Katarzyna; Pietrala, Dawid & Aperliński, Grzegorz (2014) *The NAD Phonotactic Calculator – an online tool to calculate cluster preference in English, Polish and other languages*. <http://wa.amu.edu.pl/nadcalc/>.

Dziubalska-Kołaczyk, Katarzyna & Weckwerth, Jarosław (2002) *Future Challenges for Natural Linguistics*. Munich: Lincom.

Fehringer, Carol (2011) Allomorphy in the German genitive. A paradigmatic account. *Zeitschrift für germanistische Linguistik* 39, 90–112.

Gagné, Christina (2009) Psycholinguistic Perspectives. In: Lieber, Rochelle & Štekauer, Pavol (eds) *The Oxford Handbook of Compounding*. Oxford: Oxford University Press, 255–271.

Heidolph, Karl Erich; Flämig, Walter & Motsch, Wolfgang (eds) (1981) *Grundzüge einer deutschen Grammatik* (Main features of German grammar). Berlin: Akademie-Verlag.

Hirsch-Wierzbicka, Ludomira (1971) *Funktionelle Belastung und Phonemkombination am Beispiel einsilbiger Wörter der deutschen Gegenwartssprache* (Functional stress and phoneme combination by the example of monosyllabic words of contemporary German). Hamburg: Buske.

Hongbo, Ji; Gagné, Christina L. & Spalding, Thomas L. (2011) Benefits and costs of lexical decomposition and semantic integration during the processing of transparent and opaque English compounds, *Journal of Memory and Language* 65, 406–430.

Hyman, Larry (2007) Where's Phonology in Typology? *Linguistic Typology* 11, 265–271.

Hyman, Larry & Plank, Frans (eds) (2018) *Phonological Typology*. Berlin: De Gruyter.

Jakobson, Roman (1962) *Selected Writings. Vol. I. Phonological Studies*. The Hague: Mouton.

Jespersen, Otto (1904) *Lehrbuch der Phonetik* (Textbook of Phonetics). Leipzig: B.G. Teubner.

Kamandulytė-Merfeldienė, Laura (2015) Morphonotactics in L1 acquisition of Lithuanian: TD vs SLI. *Eesti Rakenduslingvistika Ühingu aastaraamat* (Estonian papers in applied linguistics) 11, 95–109.

Kilani-Schoch, Marianne & Dressler, Wolfgang U. (2005) Morphologie naturelle et flexion du verbe francais (Natural morphology and French verb inflection). Tübingen: Narr.

Kluge, Friedrich & Götze, Alfred (1957) *Etymologisches Wörterbuch der Deutschen Sprache* (Etymological dictionary of the German language). Berlin: de Gruyter.

Korecky-Kröll Katharina; Dressler, Wolfgang U.; Freiberger, Eva M.; Reinisch, Eva; Mörth, Karlheinz & Libben, Gary (2014) Morphonotactic and phonotactic processing in German-speaking adults, *Language Sciences* 46, 48–58.

Lang, Ewald & Zifonun, Gisela (ed.) (1996) *Deutsch – typologisch* (German – typological). Berlin: de Gruyter.

Libben, Gary (1998) Semantic transparency in the processing of compounds: consequences for representation, processing, and impairment, *Brain and Language* 61, 30–44.

Luschützky, Hans Christian (1992) *Zur Phonologie der Affrikaten* (The phonology of affricates). Frankfurt: Hector.

Maddieson, Ian (2006) Correlating phonological complexity: data and validation, *Linguistic Typology* 10, 106–123.

Maddieson, Ian (2013) Consonant Inventories. In: Dryer, Matthew S. & Haspelmath, Martin (eds) *The World Atlas of Language Structures Online*. Leipzig: Max Planck Institute for Evolutionary Anthropology. <http://wals.info/chapter/1> (23 April 2018).

Mathesius, Vilém (1928) On linguistic characterology with illustration from modern English, *Actes du Premier congres international de linguistes à la Haye du 10–15 avril* 1928: 56–63.

McEnery, Tony & Hardie, Andrew (2012) *Corpus Linguistics: Method, Theory and Practice*. Cambridge University Press.

Meinhold, Gottfried & Stock, Eberhard (1980) *Phonologie der deutschen Gegenwartssprache* (Phonology of contemporary German). Leipzig: Bibliographisches Institut.

Ohala, John J. (1990) The phonetics and phonology of aspects of assimilation. In: Kingston, John & Beckman Mary E. (eds) *Papers in Laboratory Phonology I*. Cambridge: Cambridge University Press, 258–275.

Oppermann, Johannes (2004) Zurück zu den Wurzeln (Back to the roots). MA thesis, University of Vienna.

Orzechowska, Paula & Wiese, Richard (2011) Reconstructing the Sonority Hierarchy, *Proceedings of the 17th International Congress of Phonetic Sciences*, Hong Kong, China, 1542–1545.

Orzechowska, Paula & Wiese, Richard (2015) Preferences and variation in word-initial phonotactics: A multi-dimensional evaluation of German and Polish, *Folia Linguistica* 49(2): 439–486.

Plag, Ingo (2014) Phonological and phonetic variability in complex words: An uncharted territory, *Rivista di Linguistica* 26, 209–228.

Ransmayr, Jutta; Mörth, Karlheinz & Matej, Ďurčo (2017) AMC (Austrian Media Corpus) – Korpusbasierte Forschungen zum österreichischen Deutsch (Corpus-based research on Austrian German). In: Resch, Claudia & Dressler, Wolfgang U. (eds) *Digitale Methoden der Korpusforschung in Österreich* (Digital methods of corpus research in Austria). Wien: Verlag der Österreichischen Akademie der Wissenschaften, 27–38.

Shosted, Ryan (2006) Correlating complexity: a typological approach, *Linguistic Typology* 10, 1–40.

Sievers, Eduard (1876) *Grundzüge der Lautphysiologie zur Einführung in das Studium der Lautlehre der indogermanischen Sprachen* (Fundamentals of sound physiology as an introduction to the study of phonology of Indo-European languages). Leipzig: Breitkopf und Hartel.

Szczepaniak, Renata (2010) Während des Flug(e)s/des Ausflug(e)s (During the flight/the excursion): German Short and Long Genitive Endings between Norm and Variation. In: Lenz, Alexandra N. & Plewnia, Albrecht (eds) *Grammar between Norm and Variation*. Frankfurt: Lang, 103–126.

Tomasello Michael (2003) *Constructing a Language: A Usage-based Theory of Language Acquisition*. Cambridge: Harvard University Press.

Trubetzkoy, Nikolaj S. (1939) *Grundzüge der Phonologie* (Main features of phonology). Prag: Travaux du Cercle Linguistique de Prague, 7.

Whitney, William D. (1865) The relation of vowel and consonant, *Journal of the American Oriental Society* 8, 277–300.

Wiese, Richard (1988) *Silbische und Lexikalische Phonologie: Studien zum Chinesischen und Deutschen* (Syllabic and lexical phonology: Studies on Chinese and German). Tübingen: Niemeyer.

Wiese, Richard (1991) Was ist extrasilbisch im Deutschen und warum? (What is extrasyllabic in German and why?), *Zeitschrift für Sprachwissenschaft* 10, 112–133.

Wiese, Richard (2000) *The Phonology of German*. Oxford: Oxford University Press.

Zimmerer, Frank; Scharinger, Mathias & Reetz, Henning (2014) Phonological and morphological constraints on German /t/-deletions, *Journal of Phonetics* 45, 64–75.

Zydorowicz, Paulina (2010) Consonant clusters across morpheme boundaries: Polish morphonotactic inventory and its acquisition, *PSiCL* 46, 565–588.

Zydorowicz Paulina; Orzechowska, Paula; Jankowski, Michał; Dziubalska-Kołaczyk, Katarzyna; Wierzchoń, Piotr & Pietrala, Dawid (2016) *Phonotactics and morphonotactics of Polish and English. Theory, description, tools and applications*. Poznań: Adam Mickiewicz University Press.

II. Morphonotactics in speech production

HANNAH LEYKUM[1]
SYLVIA MOOSMÜLLER[†,1]

1. INTRODUCTION

The interaction between morphology and phonetics is an area for which a lot of research is still needed (see e.g. Kawahara 2011). Some findings favour the view that morphology does not influence speech production, while others indicate that an interaction between morphology and phonetics exists, i.e. there is an impact of morphology on the phonetic realization of speech.

One way to investigate this topic is to compare consonant combinations across word-internal morpheme boundaries (morphonotactic consonant clusters, e.g. /xt/ in German /mɑx+t/ *macht* '(s/he) makes'), with consonant combinations within a single morpheme (phonotactic consonant clusters, e.g. /xt/ in German /mɑxt/ *Macht* 'power'). Some consonant combinations only exist across morpheme boundaries (purely morphonotactic clusters, e.g. /xst/ in German /mɑx+st/ *machst* '(you) make'), whilst others exist nearly only within morphemes (predominantly phonotactic clusters, e.g. /mp͡f/ in German /ʃtʁʊmp͡f/ *Strumpf* 'sock'). There are, however, several consonant combinations which occur both within morphemes as well as across morpheme boundaries ((mor)phonotactic clusters); these have been studied in the present paper. For purely morphonotactic and predominantly phonotactic clusters, the cluster itself can mark the presence or absence of a morpheme boundary. However, (mor)phonotactic clusters have no boundary-signalling function. Hence, the question arises of whether morpheme boundaries within consonant clusters are marked phonetically. In order to investigate this question, the present study analyses (mor)phonotactic consonant clusters in homophonous word pairs, in word pairs of the same grammatical category, in different positions within the target words (word-final and word-medial clusters) and in languages/varieties with different typological classifications (word language, mixed-type language and quantifying language).[2]

[1] Acoustics Research Institute, Austrian Academy of Sciences, Vienna.

[2] Subsets of the material analysed in this paper have already been analysed for conference contributions and proceedings (Leykum, Moosmüller & Dressler 2015a;

2. STATE OF RESEARCH

2.1. Influence of morphology on speech production

The few studies reporting an impact of morpheme boundaries on the phonetic realization of spoken language show diverging results. Some studies indicate an impact by a morpheme boundary on speech production: several studies (Neu 1980; Guy 1991; Guy 1996; Guy, Hay & Walker 2008; Myers 1995) on word-final /t, d/-deletion in American English (AE) and New Zealand English revealed that there are fewer coronal stop deletions when /d/ represents the regular past ending of conjugated verbs. Equally, for Standard Dutch, Schuppler et al. (2012) found fewer deletions of word-final /t/ when it constitutes a morpheme. Concerning word-final /s, z/ in AE, Seyfarth (2016) spotted longer durations for the stem and suffix of inflected verbs compared to the equivalent durational measurements for uninflected homophonous words (Pluymaekers et al. 2010). The above-mentioned findings, namely fewer reductions and fewer deletions across morpheme boundaries, can be explained by the importance of highlighting the morpheme boundary in order to enhance the comprehensibility. Other studies, however, reported an influence of morphology where the direction of the effect is opposed to the aforementioned findings: Plag (2014) reported shorter durations of word-final /s/ following a morpheme boundary for Dutch. Pluymaekers et al. (2010) found an influence of morphology on the phonetic realization of the Dutch suffix *–igheid* (/əxhɛi̯t/): the cluster /xh/ is realized with a longer duration when it consists of only one morpheme; it is realized with a shorter duration when the suffix is bimorphemic (the authors explain this result by the Morphological Informativeness Hypothesis).

Contrary to these findings, other studies revealed no effect of morpheme boundaries on consonant realizations: Zimmerer, Scharinger and Reetz (2011, 2014) showed a large influence of the phonological context on the realization of word-final /t/ in German, but no influence of the morphological status of /t/. Equally, a study investigating realizations and

Leykum, Moosmüller & Dressler 2015b; Leykum & Moosmüller 2015; Leykum & Moosmüller 2016; Leykum & Moosmüller 2017; Leykum & Moosmüller 2018; Leykum & Moosmüller 2019). References concerning the corresponding papers or abstracts will be given at relevant points. However, in the present paper, a broad and detailed analysis of phonotactic and morphonotactic consonant clusters in speech production is conducted, going far beyond a summary of previous studies on subsets of the speech material.

deletions of word-final /t, d/ in British English (BE) found a high impact of the surrounding phonemes on the realizations or deletions of /t, d/, but no influence due to morphology (Tagliamonte & Temple 2005). Seyfarth (2016) investigated AE homophones and found, for stimuli ending in [t, d], no influence of a morpheme boundary prior to the final stop on stem duration or suffix duration.

Some studies investigated articulatory processes during the realization of speech segments across morpheme boundaries. Cho (2001) investigated intergestural timing across morpheme boundaries in Korean by means of electromagnetic articulography (EMA) and electropalatography (EPG). He revealed that articulation is more stable in monomorphemes and more variable across word-internal morpheme boundaries (in non-lexicalized compounds) as well as across word boundaries. However, by using combined acoustic-articulatory investigation methods (EMA, EPG, laryngography), Nakamura (2015) detected only an influence of the phonological context, but no impact of morphology on the realization or deletion of word-final coronal stops in British English.

2.2. Aim of the study and hypothesis

Until now, acoustic investigations concerning the influence of morpheme boundaries on consonant realizations have been limited to durational measurements in a few languages. The present study not only investigates two languages in which the phonotactic-morphonotactic distinction of consonant clusters has not yet been investigated (apart from our own studies) but also adds the investigation of intensity measurements to the analyses of durational measurements. In addition, contrary to most of the aforementioned studies, which analysed single consonants following morpheme boundaries, our study focuses on phonologically homophonous (mor)phonotactic consonant clusters.

Apart from speech production, other research areas have studied phonotactic and morphonotactic consonant clusters. The processing of morphonotactic clusters is assumed to be facilitated by the morphological function of the consonant clusters (Korecky-Kröll et al. 2014; Celata et al. 2015). In computer simulations, different cognitive representations for the two types of clusters have been revealed (Calderone et al. 2014). Concerning first language acquisition, the findings are mixed. Some studies found that children learn to produce morphonotactic consonant clusters earlier compared to phonotactic consonant clusters (Kamandulytė 2006; Zydorowicz 2007), while others concluded that children learn both types of clusters at the same time (Freiberger 2007). The aforementioned investigations point out that in speech processing, computer simulations, and language acquisition, differences between the two types of clusters could exist. Therefore, as an extension of the Strong Morphonotactic Hypothesis (Dressler & Dziubalska-Kołaczyk 2006), which is restricted to an interaction between morphology and phonology (not phonetics), the hypothesis of the present study predicts that these differences also exist in speech production, even though the rare findings on speech production are mixed. The hypothesis is as follows:

Consonant clusters across word-internal morpheme boundaries (morphonotactic clusters) are expected to be more robust and more highlighted in speech production than consonant clusters within a morpheme (phonotactic clusters).

Since language-specific differences are possible, three different language types are compared in the present study: a word language (Standard German German (SGG)), a mixed-type language (Standard Austrian German (SAG)) and a quantifying language (Standard French (FR)). These three types were chosen to investigate whether language-type-specific timing characteristics have an influence on the highlighting/reduction of consonant clusters. In quantifying languages, a distinction between homophonous phonotactic and morphonotactic clusters may disturb the temporal pattern of the language (Moosmüller & Brandstätter 2014). Thus, reductions of phonotactic clusters and/or lengthening of phonemes in morphonotactic clusters are expected to be less probable in quantifying languages. Therefore, with regard to the language type, it is hypothesized that durational differences between phonotactic and morphonotactic clusters will be more pronounced in SGG as compared to SAG, and the differences are expected to be greater for both varieties of German than those in FR.

2.3. Material and general methods

Stimuli

Comparisons of the acoustic characteristics of consonant clusters within morphemes and across word-internal morpheme boundaries are only conclusive when the clusters are phonologically homophonous. Therefore, for the present study, several (mor)phonotactic consonant clusters were chosen which occur in the same position within words, once as a phonotactic cluster, and once as a morphonotactic cluster (emerging from productive word-formation rules). Since morphonotactic consonant clusters in the word-initial position are not possible in German, only consonant clusters in a word-medial and word-final position were considered for the present investigation.

The target words were nouns, verbs, and adjectives with a (mor)phonotactic consonant cluster in a word-final or word-medial position. Within each word pair, the phonemes preceding and (for word-medial clusters) following the consonant cluster were kept as constant as possible to minimize the influence of the phonological context on the realization of the consonant cluster. Therefore, the target words with word-final consonant clusters were pairs of homophonous words, which raises the problem that we have to compare nouns and conjugated verbs. For the target words with word-medial consonant clusters, word pairs belonging to the same grammatical category were chosen. The target words are listed in Table 1. Since the word pairs were not matched for word frequency, this variable was controlled for statistically. Word frequency values were extracted from http://wortschatz.uni-leipzig.de (Quasthoff, Goldhahn & Heyer 2013).

Participants

Recordings of 16 speakers of Standard Austrian German (SAG) were made. All these SAG speakers were, as defined by Moosmüller (1991), students (younger age group) or university graduates (younger and older age group) who were born and raised in Vienna, with at least one parent fulfilling the same criteria. The speakers can be assigned to two equal age groups: the younger speakers were between 18 and 25 years old; the older speakers were 45–60 years old. In both age groups, the speakers were balanced for gender.

Additionally, recordings of six younger speakers (18–25 years) of Standard French (FR) and eight speakers (18–25 years) of Standard German German (SGG) were conducted. In both groups, the speakers were balanced for gender. The speakers of FR were students or university graduates originating from the region Île-de-France; all speakers of SGG were born and raised in the northern part of Germany (north of the Benrath line). For all participants, the same criteria were fulfilled by at least one parent.

Recordings

The recordings were conducted in a semi-anechoic sound booth (IAC-1202A). In the recording session, after a semi-structured interview, the participants undertook several reading tasks. For one reading task, the target words were embedded in carrier phrases in a post-focal position. For this, the participants were told that they had to correct a misunderstanding concerning the addressee of an utterance. In the sentences, the pronoun or name was printed in bold, and the participants were asked to stress the pronoun/name when reading the sentences. This type of carrier phrase and the corresponding instructions were chosen to avoid stress on the target word, to enable phonetic reduction processes. The target word was always followed by the word *gesagt* 'said' to control the following phonological context for words with a word-final consonant cluster. The sentence finished with *glaube ich* 'I think' to avoid a sentence-final lengthening starting already in the target word. The following sentences are two examples of sentences for the first reading task:

Zu ***ihr****? - Ich habe zu* ***ihm*** *„die Hast" gesagt, glaube ich.*

'To **her**? - I said to **him** "the hurry", I think.'

Zu ***mir****? - Ich habe zu* ***Peter*** *„er macht" gesagt, glaube ich.*

'To **me**? - I said to **Peter** "he makes", I think.'

In a second speaking task, semi-spontaneous speech was elicited. In this task, the speakers had to read a given question (in which the target word was already mentioned) and answer the question by including two given words in their answer. The first given word was the target word, and the second word was given to draw attention away from the target word and to facilitate the task. Only SAG and FR speakers performed the semi-spontaneous task. Here are two examples of the semi-spontaneous speaking task:

Hast, Schlüssel	*Was vergisst dein Nachbar oft in der Hast mitzunehmen?*
'hurry, keys'	'What does your neighbour often forget when he is in a hurry?'
hasst, Katzen	*Hasst Herr Müller Hunde?*
'hates, cats'	'Does Mr. Müller hate dogs?'

Possible answers by the participants for the first question were: *In der Hast vergisst er seine Schlüssel* 'When he is in a hurry, he forgets his keys', and for the second example: *Nein, Herr Müller hasst Katzen* 'No, Mr. Müller hates cats'.

Additionally, some of the target words with word-final consonant clusters were embedded in more natural sentences. In this, for the target words, which were verbs, the subject pronoun and the verb were separated to reduce the redundant coding of the morpheme boundary. In addition, the target word was always followed by a word starting with /g/, to reduce the impact of the phonological context. These sentences were only read by the speakers of SAG. Two examples of this second reading task are given below:

Die Zeit misst gleich in der nächsten Runde Matthias.
'The time will be measured in the next round by Matthias.'

Ihr Freund hat gesagt, dass er sie nicht wirklich hasst, glaube ich.
'Her friend said that he does not really hate her, I think.'

For both reading tasks, the sentences were put in random order and read by the participants twice within the larger recording session. The semi-spontaneous speaking task was conducted only once. After subtracting a few mispronounced and misread items, this resulted in a total of 2,402 analysable target words (SAG + SGG + FR; word-medial + word-final).

In order to conduct the acoustic analyses, the recordings were manually segmented and annotated with STx (Noll et al. 2007) on a sentence, word and phoneme level. The duration and intensity values of the following segments were measured and semi-automatically extracted: target words, surrounding words, consonant clusters, individual consonants of the clusters, and phonemes surrounding the clusters.

The data was statistically analysed with R (R Core Team 2015) by using mixed-effects models (Bates et al. 2015). The variables subject and word were included in the models as random factors. Additionally, the following control variables were included in the models whenever they had an effect on the dependent variables: word frequency, articulation rate, /t/-deletions, stress on the target word, and pauses following the target word.

The mixed-effects models were fitted using a forward approach: effects were added one by one. Based on the p-value, a decision was made on whether to keep the variable or interaction in the model or to exclude it (threshold: $p = 0.1$). Where necessary, Tukey post-hoc tests with p-value adjustment were carried out.

To normalize the data, two different methods were used: on the one hand, the total duration (or mean syllable duration for word-medial clusters) or intensity of the target word were included in the statistical analyses to control statistically for any impact of speaker-specific differences. On the other hand, the relative duration of each cluster or consonant was calculated by dividing the segment duration by the word duration, cluster duration or mean syllable duration (for word-medial clusters). To calculate the relative intensity, the intensity of the segment was divided by the mean word intensity or cluster intensity. The normalization method used for each analysis is indicated in the following section.

Table 1. Target words (translations are provided in Table 2 and Table 4)

	SAG word-final		SAG word-medial		SGG		French	
Cluster	morphonotactic	phonotactic	morphonotactic	phonotactic	morphonotactic	phonotactic	morphonotactic	phonotactic
/ft/	*schafft*	*Schaft*			*schafft*	*Schaft*		
/xt/	*macht*	*Macht*	*Frachter*	*Fachtagung*	*macht*	*Macht*		
/pst/	*probst*	*Propst*						
/ŋkst/	*hängst*	*Hengst*			*hängst*	*Hengst*		
/nt/	*rinnt*	*Rind*						
/nst/	*dienst*	*Dienst*						
/st/	*misst*	*Mist*	*passte*	*Paste*	*misst*	*Mist*		
	hasst	*Hast*	*küsste*	*Küste*	*hasst*	*Hast*		
/ŋkt/			*Funkturm*	*Akupunktur*				
/sm/			*verhältnismäßig*	*kosmetisch*	*verhältnismäßig*	*kosmetisch*	*transmission*	*cosmétique*
			Missmut	*Organismus*	*Missmut*	*Organismus*		
/sl/			*löslich*	*isländisch*	*löslich*	*isländisch*	*dislocation*	*islandaise*
			häuslich	*islamisch*	*häuslich*	*islamisch*		
/sk/			*diskontinuierlich*	*Diskothek*	*diskontinuierlich*	*Diskothek*	*discontinu(e)*	*discothèque*
/ksp/			*Expartner*	*Experte*	*Expartner*	*Experte*	*expatrier*	*expert*
			Fixpunkt	*Experiment*	*Fixpunkt*	*Experiment*		

3. ACOUSTIC ANALYSES

3.1. Word-final clusters in SAG and SGG

First, word-final consonant clusters in homophonous word pairs realized by speakers of SAG (16 speakers) and SGG (8 young speakers) were compared (see also Leykum & Moosmüller 2015, Leykum et al. 2015a, Leykum & Moosmüller 2016). The target words were realized by all speakers twice within the carrier phrases. Moreover, the speakers of SAG conducted two additional tasks: they read sentences in which the subject pronoun and verb were separated for the bimorphemic target words (twice), and they realized the target word once in the semi-spontaneous speaking task.

The investigated target words were the following:

Table 2. Target words with word-final consonant cluster[3]

	SAG		SGG	
Cluster	phonotactic	morphonotactic	phonotactic	morphonotactic
/ft/	*Schaft* 'stem'	*schafft* '(s/he) creates'	*Schaft* 'stem'	*schafft* '(s/he) creates'
/xt/	*Macht* 'power'	*macht* '(s/he) makes'	*Macht* 'power'	*macht* '(s/he) makes'
/pst/	*Propst* 'provost'	*probst* '(you) rehearse'		
/ŋkst/	*Hengst* 'stallion'	*hängst* '(you) hang'	*Hengst* 'stallion'	*hängst* '(you) hang'
/nst/	*Dienst* 'service'	*dienst* '(you) serve'		
/nt/ /nd̥/	*Rind* 'beef, cow'	*rinnt* '(it) flows'		
/st/	*Mist* 'dung, rubbish' *Hast* 'hurry'	*misst* '(s/he) measures' *hasst* '(s/he) hates'	*Mist* 'dung, rubbish' *Hast* 'hurry'	*misst* '(s/he) measures' *hasst* '(s/he) hates'

[3] Even though the orthography differs, for all word pairs, the item with a phonotactic cluster and its counterpart with a morphonotactic cluster are phonemically homophonous.

Results

/t/-deletion

In the word-final position, /t/ was acoustically deleted in several cases. In total, /t/-deletions occurred in 11.18% of the phonotactic clusters, whereas in morphonotactic clusters, 13.64% of word-final /t/ were acoustically deleted. The deletion rates did not significantly differ between the two types of clusters (z = -0.877, p = 0.381). Since the deletion rate is highly influenced by the phonological context ($z = 3.777, p < 0.001$), only the /t/s followed by /g/ were regarded in the next step. Out of these clusters, 11.16% of the phonotactic clusters were realized without the /t/, and 10.38% of the morphonotactic clusters (here again, there is no significant difference between the two types of clusters: z = -0.220, p = 0.826).

Concerning the segmental context, the deletion rate of /t/ was highest when the preceding phoneme was the homorganic fricative /s/ as compared to the other preceding contexts (z = -4.139, $p < 0.001$; /t/-deletions following /s/: 16.09% in phonotactic clusters, 16.23% in morphonotactic clusters; /t/-deletions following other phonemes: 3.36% in phonotactic clusters, 7.66% in morphonotactic clusters, see Figure 1).

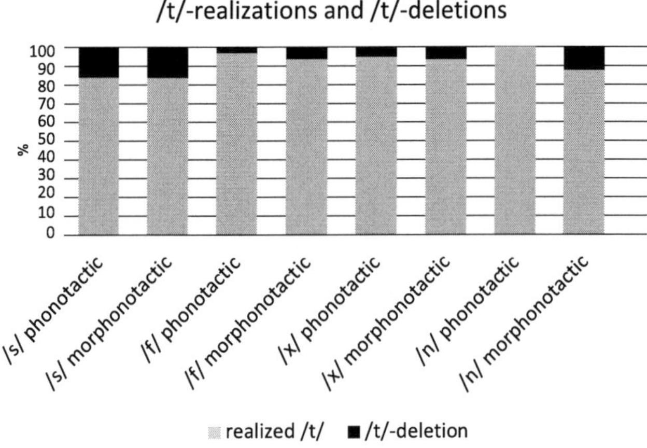

Figure 1. Percentages of /t/-realizations and /t/-deletions

Relative duration of the cluster

The fitted mixed-effects models revealed the following significant effects for the relative duration of the entire cluster (in % of word duration): a type-of-cluster*speaking-task interaction (F(2,1383) = 20.800,

$p < 0.001$), a type-of-cluster*/t/-realization interaction ($t(1398) = 3.210$, $p = 0.001$), a gender*variety/age interaction ($F(2,18) = 3.940$, $p = 0.037$), a main effect of articulation rate ($t(1395) = -10.670$, $p < 0.001$), and a main effect of the cluster ($F(6,7) = 47.035$, $p < 0.001$). Post-hoc analyses showed a significant type-of-cluster difference for the type-of-cluster*speaking-task interaction in the additional speaking task only, where subject pronoun and conjugated verb were separated. Here, the phonotactic clusters were shorter compared to the morphonotactic clusters ($t(24) = 3.629$, $p = 0.015$). The type-of-cluster*/t/-realization interaction revealed shorter durations for both types of clusters when the word-final /t/ was deleted. This effect was slightly larger for morphonotactic clusters (phonotactic: $t(1408) = 6.723$, $p < 0.001$; morphonotactic: $t(1411) = 11.539$, $p < 0.001$, see Figure 2). A closer look at the gender*variety/age interaction revealed that the clusters of the elder female SAG-speakers were shorter compared to all other groups of speakers (see Table 3).

Table 3. Gender*variety/age-interaction (post-hoc tests)

contrast	df	t-value	p-value	significance
SAG: elder, female – SAG: elder, male	16.89	-3.752	0.0168	*
SAG: elder, female – SAG: young, female	18.11	-2.950	0.0776	.
SAG: elder, female – SAG: young, male	18.09	-3.184	0.0493	*
SAG: elder, female – SGG: young, female	23.60	-4.320	0.0029	**
SAG: elder, female – SGG: young, male	22.64	-4.687	0.0013	**

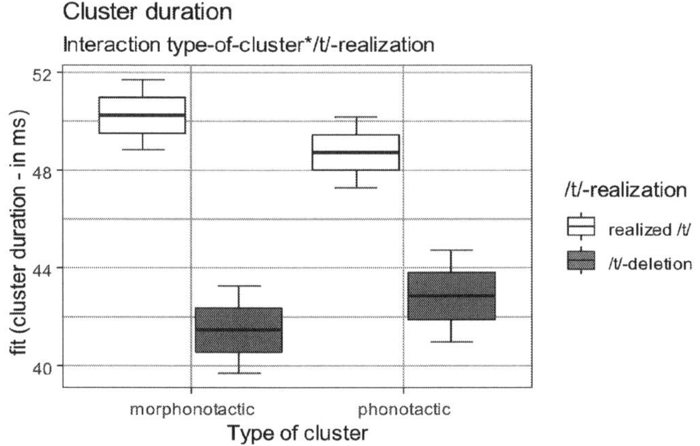

Figure 2. Interaction type-of-cluster*/t/-realization

Relative duration of /t/

Concerning the duration of /t/ in relation to the duration of the entire word (% of word duration), the statistical analyses revealed a significant three-way interaction between the task, the word frequency and the type of cluster ($F(2,1194) = 5.291$, $p = 0.005$), and main effects of articulation rate ($t(1114) = 2.641$, $p = 0.008$), variety/age (tendency: $F(2,20) = 2.909$, $p = 0.077$; elder SAG < younger SAG < SGG speakers), gender (tendency: $t(19) = 1.994$, $p = 0.061$; female < male speakers), and cluster ($F(6,7) = 17.111$, $p < 0.001$). Post-hoc analyses showed that only for the speaking task with separated pronoun and verb was it the case that the higher the word frequency, the more the two types of clusters differed in their length; with /t/ being relatively longer in morphonotactic clusters (see Figure 3).

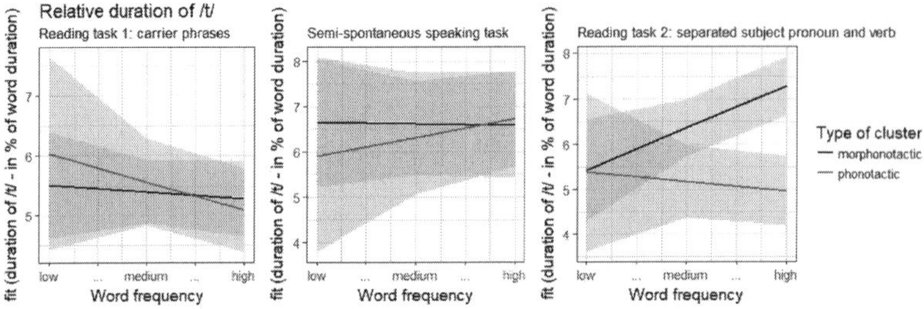

Figure 3. Three-way interaction: task*word-frequency*type-of-cluster

The effect of the articulation rate (longer relative duration of /t/ for higher articulation rates) emerged due to an articulation rate-induced shortening of the entire word (especially the vowel: main effect of articulation rate ($t(1230) = -8.621$, $p < 0.001$).

Relative intensity of the clusters

The fitted mixed-effects model showed that the relative intensity of the clusters (in % of word intensity) is significantly influenced by an interaction between the task and /t/-realization ($F(2,1406) = 4.114$, $p = 0.016$), a word-frequency*articulation-rate interaction ($t(1397) = -2.780$, $p = 0.005$), a main effect of gender ($t(22) = 3.562$, $p = 0.002$), and a main effect of cluster ($F(6,9) = 130$, $p < 0.001$). No influence of the type of cluster was found ($p = 0.804$). A post-hoc test concerning the task*/t/-realization interaction revealed significantly lower relative cluster intensities of clusters with realized final /t/ compared to the clusters with

/t/-deletion for both reading tasks (carrier phrases: $t(1409) = -3.215$, $p = 0.017$; second reading task: $t(1401) = -3.659$, $p = 0.004$), but not for the semi-spontaneous speaking task ($t(1402) = -0.237$, $p = 0.999$).

Relative intensity of /t/

The relative intensity of /t/ (in % of word intensity) is influenced by an interaction between the type of cluster and the task ($F(2,1122) = 6.657$, $p = 0.001$), an interaction of task and gender ($F(2,1204) = 9.462$, $p < 0.001$), a main effect of articulation rate ($t(1213) = 2.989$, $p = 0.003$), and a main effect of cluster ($F(6,12) = 13.959$, $p < 0.001$). Post-hoc analyses revealed that in none of the speaking tasks did phonotactic and morphonotactic clusters differ in their relative intensity of /t/. However, the relative intensity of /t/ was significantly lower in the speaking task with a separated subject pronoun and verb as compared to /t/ in target words embedded in the carrier phrases. This effect was slightly larger for the phonotactic clusters (morphonotactic clusters: $t(1204) = 4.058$, $p < 0.001$; phonotactic clusters: $t(1147) = 7.607$, $p < 0.001$, see Figure 4).

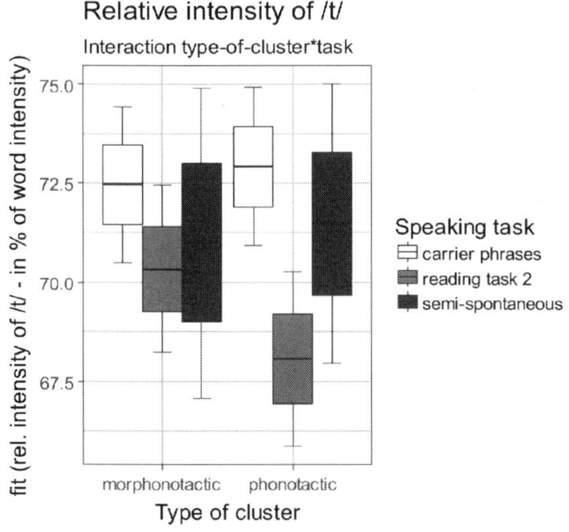

Figure 4. Interaction type-of-cluster*task

Discussion of word-final consonant clusters

Regarding the number of acoustic deletions of /t/ and the relative intensity of the cluster, no significant difference between phonotactic and morphonotactic clusters exists. For the other investigated variables, interactions including an effect of the type of cluster reached significance. However, no main effects of the type of cluster were found. The interactions were, with one exception, all interactions with the speaking task. The additional speaking task was designed to test whether the redundant coding of the information given by the conjugational morpheme reduces the importance of a highlighting of the morpheme boundary, which could result in less highlighting of morphonotactic clusters. Therefore, opposing effects could explain the lack of a difference between the phonetic realization of phonotactic and morphonotactic clusters in the other speaking tasks. However, the effects of the present study could not be interpreted as evidence for this hypothesis, since the additional speaking task involved a highly unnatural wording for some of the sentences, which in itself results in a higher articulation accuracy. The target words containing phonotactic clusters were also embedded in the sentences. For the nouns, however, the context was more natural, possibly resulting in a less accurate articulation. In addition, some of the target words with a morphonotactic cluster were in a phrase-final position, resulting in phrase-final lengthening of the target word.

With regard to the relative duration of the cluster, the type-of-cluster*/t/-realization interaction showing a slightly larger difference between clusters with and without final /t/ for morphonotactic clusters compared to phonotactic clusters seems to be a random result, which possibly emerged due to differences between the clusters themselves and the low number of clusters with /t/-deletion.

The effects of the type of cluster emerging in the analyses can easily be explained by the unnatural wording, and by differences in the positions of the target words within the sentences in the second reading task. However, when investigating word-final consonant clusters in German homophones, the lack of an effect of a cluster-internal morpheme boundary on speech production could not be interpreted as evidence for the non-existence of an influence of the morpheme boundary on the realization of morphonotactic consonant clusters. Within each word pair, the stimuli not only differed in being monomorphemic or bimorphemic, but also in the grammatical category to which the target words belong.

3.2. Word-medial clusters in SAG, SGG and FR

In a further step, the (mor)phonotactic clusters in word-medial position were investigated (see Leykum & Moosmüller (2019) for word-medial clusters in SAG; Leykum & Moosmüller (2017) for a comparison of the three languages/varieties). Here, in most cases, the grammatical category was identical for both stimuli within each word pair. The target words are listed in Table 4.

Table 4. Target words with word-medial consonant cluster (p = phonotactic, m = morphonotactic; the word pairs not matched for grammatical category are shaded)

	SAG word-medial		SGG		French	
Cluster	p	m	p	m	p	m
/st/	*Paste* 'paste'	*passte* '(it) fitted'				
	Küste 'coast'	*küsste* '(s/he) kissed'				
/xt/	*Frachter* 'cargo ship'	*Fachtagung* 'symposium'				
/ŋkt/	*Akupunktur* 'acupuncture'	*Funkturm* 'radio tower'				
/sm/	*kosmetisch* 'cosmetic'	*verhältnismäßig* 'relative'	*kosmetisch* 'cosmetic'	*verhältnismäßig* 'relative'	*cosmétique* 'cosmetic'	*transmission* 'transmission'
	Organismus 'organism'	*Missmut* 'displeasure'	*Organismus* 'organism'	*Missmut* 'displeasure'		
/sl/	*isländisch* 'Icelandic'	*löslich* 'soluble'	*isländisch* 'Icelandic'	*löslich* 'soluble'	*islandaise* 'Icelandic'	*dislocation* 'dislocation'
	islamisch 'Islamic'	*häuslich* 'domestic'	*islamisch* 'Islamic'	*häuslich* 'domestic'		
/sk/	*Diskothek* 'discotheque'	*diskontinuierlich* 'discontinuous'	*Diskothek* 'discotheque'	*diskontinuierlich* 'discontinuous'	*discothèque* 'discotheque'	*discontinue* 'discontinuous'

/ksp/	*Experte* 'expert'	*Expartner* 'ex-part-ner'	*Experte* 'expert'	*Expartner* 'ex-part-ner'	*expert* 'expert'	*expatrier* 'expatriate'
	Experi-ment 'experi-ment'	*Fixpunkt* 'fixed point'	*Experiment* 'experi-ment'	*Fixpunkt* 'fixed point'		

The target words were realized twice by all 30 speakers (16 SAG, 8 SGG, 6 FR) within the carrier phrases. In addition, the speakers of SAG and FR conducted the semi-spontaneous speaking task.

Results

Absolute cluster duration

The statistical analyses (with relative syllable duration as the control variable) showed a significant interaction between language/variety and articulation rate ($F(3,753)$=9.863, p<0.001), an interaction between articulation rate and cluster ($F(6,918) = 11.944$, $p < 0.001$), and a main effect of the speaking task ($t(912) = -3.018$, $p = 0.003$; shorter clusters in the semi-spontaneous speaking task). Concerning the language/variety*articulation-rate interaction, a decrease in the cluster duration with increasing articulation rate was slightly steeper for the speakers of SGG compared to the other groups of speakers. The articulation-rate*cluster interaction emerged because the duration of the clusters /ŋkt/ and /ksp/ was more affected by the articulation rate than the other clusters. The duration of the cluster /sk/ was least influenced by the articulation rate. A morpheme boundary within the clusters had no influence on the duration of the clusters ($p = 0.864$).

Since the material is not well balanced, another mixed-effects model was fitted for a subset of the data. Here, only the stimuli embedded in the carrier phrases were analysed. Furthermore, the French items and the word pairs *Paste-passte* 'paste-fitted', *Küste-küsste* 'coast-kissed' and *Diskothek-diskontinuierlich* 'discotheque-discontinuous' were excluded so that only word pairs matched for their grammatical category were used, to enhance the comparability. For this subset of data, a three-way interaction between gender, type of cluster and grammatical category emerged ($F(1,463) = 7.398$, $p = 0.007$). Post-hoc analyses showed longer durations of phonotactic clusters for both genders for adjectives. Concerning nouns, no effect occurred for female speakers. For male speakers, however, the phonotactic clusters were shorter compared to the clusters of female speakers and compared to male speakers producing morphonotactic clusters (see Figure 5). An articulation-rate*cluster interaction ($F(4,470) = 5.970$, $p < 0.001$) revealed the same effects as the analyses of the entire dataset (see above). In addition, an effect of variety/age ($F(2,12) = 21.320$, $p < 0.001$) revealed that speakers of SGG produced the clusters with longer durations compared to both age groups of speakers of SAG.

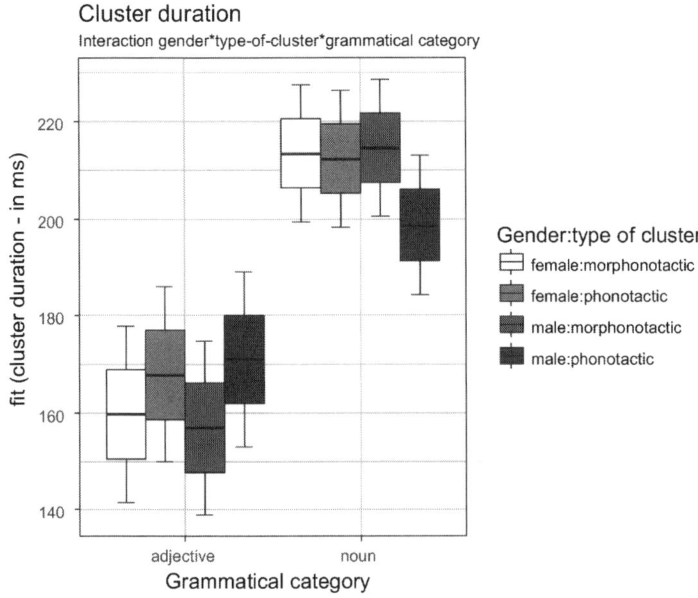

Figure 5. Interaction gender*type-of-cluster*grammatical category

Relative cluster duration (in % of mean syllable duration)

When normalizing the cluster duration by using the mean syllable duration, the fitted mixed-effects model showed the following significant effects: a task*articulation-rate interaction ($F(1,878) = 9.315$, $p = 0.002$), a main effect of language/variety ($F(3,24) = 7.962$, $p < 0.001$), and a main effect of cluster ($F(6,21) = 3.210$, $p = 0.021$). A morpheme boundary within the cluster had no effect on the relative duration of word-medial clusters ($p = 0.461$).

Duration of the cluster-final consonant relative to the cluster duration

When dividing the clusters at the position of the morpheme boundary of the morphonotactic clusters (/xt/ → /x+t/, /ŋkt/ → /ŋk+t/, /sm/ → /s+m/, /sl/ → /s+l/, /sk/ → /s+k/, /ksp/ → /ks+p/) and dividing the duration of the second part of the cluster by the total cluster duration, the relative duration of the cluster-final consonant is calculated. The statistical analyses revealed that the relative duration of the cluster-final consonant is influenced by an interaction between articulation rate, gender and task ($F(1,868) = 4.014$, $p = 0.045$): for target words in carrier phrases, the relative duration of the cluster-final consonant is influenced by the articulation rate only for female speakers. In the semi-spontaneous speaking task, the articulation rate does not influence the duration of the cluster-final consonant. In addition, a main effect of cluster ($F(6,20) = 7.800$, $p < 0.001$) occurred. The type of cluster had no influence on the relative duration of the cluster-final consonant ($p = 0.307$). When reducing the data to a subset of the stimuli which were balanced in terms of the grammatical category, a tendency for an effect of the grammatical category ($F(2,19) = 4.723$, $p = 0.059$) showed longer durations for the cluster-final consonant in adjectives compared to nouns. However, this is not a global effect of differences between nouns and adjectives, but more likely an effect arising due to differences between the different word pairs.

Absolute intensity of the cluster

The absolute intensity of the investigated word-medial consonant clusters is influenced by a main effect of gender ($t(22) = 2.929$, $p = 0.008$), with higher intensity of the clusters realized by male speakers. In addition, a main effect of cluster ($F(6,22) = 20.900$, $p < 0.001$) occurred, and a main effect of speaking task ($t(925) = 3.890$, $p < 0.001$), with higher intensities in the semi-spontaneous speaking task. The type of cluster had no significant influence on the absolute intensity of the clusters ($p = 0.125$).

Relative intensity of the cluster (relative to the intensity of the vowel preceding the cluster)

When normalizing the cluster intensity by calculating the intensity in relation to the intensity of the vowel preceding the cluster, besides an effect of cluster ($F(6,19) = 9.128$, $p < 0.001$), a significant three-way interaction between word-frequency*articulation-rate*language/variety ($F(3,920) = 5.794, p < 0.001$) occurred. In this, for the speakers of SGG, the relative intensity of the clusters decreased with increasing word frequency for higher articulation rates. The other groups of speakers did not show such an effect. Here again, the type of cluster did not influence the intensity values of the clusters ($p = 0.133$).

Intensity of the cluster-final consonant relative to the cluster intensity

The relative intensity of the cluster-final consonant was calculated by dividing the intensity of the consonant by the intensity of the cluster. The fitted mixed-effects model resulted in a main effect of language/variety ($F(3,24) = 5.039, p = 0.008$), a main effect of cluster ($F(6,21) = 87.051, p < 0.001$), and a main effect of task ($t(938) = 3.727, p < 0.001$). Post-hoc analyses showed that the relative intensity of the cluster-final consonant is lower in FR compared to SAG and SGG. In addition, it is higher in the semi-spontaneous speaking task. The effect of language/variety emerged due to language- and item-specific word-stress differences. The type of cluster had no influence on the relative intensity of the cluster-final consonant ($p = 0.118$).

Discussion of word-medial consonant clusters

One advantage of investigating word-medial clusters is the possibility to compare word pairs of the same grammatical category, as well as to compare French and German consonant clusters, as some consonant clusters exist in both languages, both within morphemes and across morpheme boundaries in a word-medial position. However, there are also several disadvantages: it is not possible to control the phonological context as much as for clusters in homophones; the target words are more diverse, not only in terms of the phonemes surrounding the consonant clusters, but also in terms of the exact position of the consonant clusters within the words, and, most importantly, in terms of the position of the word stress within the German target words.

In order to investigate the impact of the grammatical category of the target words on the realization of the consonant clusters, the dataset was restricted to a subset including only word pairs where both items within each pair belong to an identical grammatical category. These analyses revealed an effect from the grammatical category in only two of the fitted models: concerning the absolute cluster duration and concerning the relative duration of the cluster-final consonant. With regard to the absolute duration of the cluster, the grammatical category was part of a three-way interaction, revealing a longer duration of phonotactic clusters for adjectives for all speakers and a shorter duration of the phonotactic clusters for nouns when realized by male speakers. Furthermore, the relative duration of the cluster-final consonant was longer in adjectives compared to nouns. Since there were no interactions between the grammatical category and the type of cluster besides the three-way interaction, it could be concluded that for adjectives and nouns, a possible influence of the grammatical category could be ruled out as a factor which could mask effects of a morpheme boundary on the realization of word-medial consonant clusters. In addition, concerning the three-way interaction affecting the absolute cluster duration, the effect on the adjectives is in the opposite direction to the hypothesis: in adjectives, phonotactic clusters were longer than morphonotactic clusters. Concerning nouns, the phonotactic clusters of male speakers were shorter compared to the other clusters, which could be interpreted as less reduction of the morphonotactic clusters by male speakers, compared to a low level of reductions by female speakers, irrespective of the presence or absence of a morpheme boundary.

Concerning all other investigated variables, no effect of a consonant cluster internal morpheme boundary on the realization of the word-medial clusters was detectable.

4. GENERAL DISCUSSION

Previous studies investigating the influence of morpheme boundaries on speech production came to different results. Some studies revealed an effect indicating an acoustic highlighting of the morpheme boundary by lengthening phonemes across morpheme boundaries. Other studies found no effect of a morpheme boundary, or even indicated results with an effect in the opposite direction. Likewise, in the present study, for some variables an effect of the type of cluster emerged, either in the expected direction or in the opposite direction. However, most analyses did not find any effect of the morpheme boundary.

Since the effects of an influence by the morpheme boundary can all be easily explained by other interfering variables, the present study is not able to give any evidence for an impact of morphology on speech production. However, the absence of any effects does not necessarily imply that no influence of morpheme boundaries on the realization of consonant clusters exists.

The possibility that the highly redundant coding of the information of the morpheme boundary in conjugated verbs with word-final morphonotactic consonant clusters leads to a less accurate articulation cannot be ruled out. Opposite effects caused by the morpheme boundary and the high redundancy are still possible. Due to the unnatural wording and the lack of a possibility to match the target words in terms of the position within the sentences, the additional reading task did not provide conclusive findings.

Another factor linked to the redundancy, described by Hanique and Ernestus (2012: 175), is the word-information load: "The less a segment contributes to distinguishing the complete word from other words, the more it may be reduced". Equally, the degree of morphological decomposability could constitute a factor influencing whether morphonotactic consonant clusters are treated differently from phonotactic clusters in speech production.

The present findings were able to rule out language- and/or variety-specific timing characteristics as a factor inhibiting an acoustic differentiation between phonotactic and morphonotactic clusters (see also Leykum & Moosmüller 2017). However, besides language-specific timing characteristics, other language-specific differences could exist. The investigated languages share a low morphological richness, raising the question of whether the morphological richness of a language determines whether phonotactic and morphonotactic clusters behave the same or not. It is possible that in morphologically richer languages, the information about the morpheme boundary is more important to ensure intelligibility. A fact supporting this hypothesis is research on first language acquisition. It was shown that children acquiring Austrian German learn both types of clusters at the same time (Freiberger 2007), whereas, in the first language acquisition of the morphologically richer languages Polish and Lithuanian, children learn to produce morphonotactic consonant clusters correctly prior to phonotactic consonant clusters (Kamandulytė 2006; Zydorowicz 2007).

5. CONCLUSION

Combining the present findings with analyses of the subsegmental parts of /t/ in word-final clusters (Leykum & Moosmüller 2015; Leykum et al. 2015b; Leykum & Moosmüller 2018), conducted on the same material, none of the analyses could prove that morphonotactic consonant clusters are more highlighted or less susceptible to reduction processes.

Yet, the present analyses do not prove that phonotactic and morphonotactic consonant clusters are identical in their phonetic realization, since statistically insignificant results do not imply that no effect exists. However, the fact that quite a lot of analyses were conducted on a relatively large dataset, all showing no or no stable effect of the morpheme boundary on speech production, leads us to the conclusion that it is very unlikely that speakers realize morphonotactic consonant clusters in German differently because of the morpheme boundary.

ACKNOWLEDGEMENTS

The current investigation was undertaken within the project I 1394-G23 'Human Behaviour and Machine Simulation in the Processing of (Mor)Phonotactics', funded by the FWF Austrian Science Fund and the project 'Die österreichische Standardaussprache Wiens in Kontakt mit der deutschen Standardaussprache', funded by Kultur Wien.

REFERENCES

Bates, Douglas; Mächler, Martin; Bolker, Ben & Walker, Steve (2015) Fitting linear mixed-effects models using lme4, *Journal of Statistical Software* 67(1), 1–48. doi:10.18637/jss.v067.i01

Calderone, Basilio; Celata, Chiara; Korecky-Kröll, Katharina & Dressler, Wolfgang U. (2014) A computational approach to morphonotactics. Evidence from German, *Language Sciences* 46, 59–70. doi:10.1016/j.langsci.2014.06.007

Celata, Chiara; Korecky-Kröll, Katharina; Ricci, Irene & Dressler, Wolfgang U. (2015) Phonotactic processing and morpheme boundaries: word-final /Cst/ clusters in German, *Italian Journal of Linguistics* 27(1), 85–110.

Cho, Taehong (2001) Effects of morpheme boundaries on intergestural timing. Evidence from Korean, *Phonetica* 58(3), 129–162. doi:10.1159/000056196

Dressler, Wolfgang U. & Dziubalska-Kołaczyk, Katarzyna (2006) Proposing morphonotactics, *Italian Journal of Linguistics* 18(2), 249–266.

Freiberger, Eva M. (2007) Morphonotaktik im Erstspracherwerb des Deutschen (Morphonotactics in first language acquisition in German), *Wiener Linguistische Gazette* 74, 1–23.

Guy, Gregory R. (1991) Contextual conditioning in variable lexical phonology, *Language Variation and Change* 3, 223–239.

Guy, Gregory R. (1996) Form and function in linguistic variation. In: Guy, Gregory R.; Feagin, Crawford; Schiffrin, Deborah & Baugh, John (eds) *Towards a Social Science of Language. Papers in Honor of William Labov. Volume 1: Variation and Change in Language and Society*. [Current Issues in Linguistic Theory]. Amsterdam/Philadelphia: John Benjamins Publishing Company, 221–252.

Guy, Gregory R; Hay, Jennifer & Walker, Abby (2008) Phonological, lexical, and frequency factors in coronal stop deletion in early New Zealand English, *Laboratory Phonology* 11, 53–54.

Hanique, Iris & Ernestus, Mirjam (2012) The role of morphology in acoustic reduction, *Lingue e Linguaggio* 2, 147–164.

Kamandulytė, Laura (2006) The acquisition of morphonotactics in Lithuanian, *Wiener Linguistische Gazette* 73, 88–96.

Kawahara, Shigeto (2011) Experimental approaches in theoretical phonology. In: van Oostendorp, Marc; Ewen, Colin J; Hume, Elizabeth & Rice, Keren (eds) *The Blackwell Companion to Phonology. Volume IV: Phonological Interfaces*. Oxford: Wiley-Blackwell, 2283–2303.

Korecky-Kröll, Katharina; Dressler, Wolfgang U; Freiberger, Eva M.; Reinisch, Eva; Mörth, Karlheinz & Libben, Gary (2014) Morphonotactic and phonotactic processing in German-speaking adults, *Language Sciences* 46, 48–58. doi:10.1016/j.langsci.2014.06.006

Leykum, Hannah; Moosmüller, Sylvia & Dressler, Wolfgang U. (2015a) Homophonous phonotactic and morphonotactic consonant clusters in word-final position. *Proceedings of the 16th annual conference of International Speech Communication Association (INTERSPEECH)*, 1685–1689.

Leykum, Hannah; Moosmüller, Sylvia & Dressler, Wolfgang U. (2015b) Word-final (mor) phonotactic consonant clusters in Standard Austrian German. *Proceedings of the 18th International Congress of Phonetic Sciences (ICPhS)*. <http://www.internationalphoneticassociation.org/icphs-proceedings/ICPhS2015/Papers/ICPHS0701.pdf>.

Leykum, Hannah & Moosmüller, Sylvia (2015) Das (mor)phonotaktische Konsonantencluster /st/ in wortmedialer und wortfinaler Position in homophonen Wortpaaren (The (mor)phontactic consonant cluster /st/ in word-medial und word-final position in homophonous word pairs). *11. Tagung Phonetik und Phonologie im deutschsprachigen Raum*, Marburg (Poster).

Leykum, Hannah & Moosmüller, Sylvia (2016) (Mor)phonotactic consonant clusters in Standard Austrian German and Standard German. *Tagungsband der 12. Tagung Phonetik und Phonologie im deutschsprachigen Raum*, 103–106. doi:10.1787/578054332028

Leykum, Hannah & Moosmüller, Sylvia (2017) Phonotactic and morphonotactic consonant clusters in Standard German German, Standard Austrian German and Standard French, *Phonetics and Phonology in Europe (PaPE 2017)*, Cologne.

Leykum, Hannah & Moosmüller, Sylvia (2018) Factors influencing the realisation of word-final /t/ in Standard Austrian German and Standard German German. In: *Proceedings of the Conference on Phonetics & Phonology in German-speaking countries (P&P 13)*. Humboldt-Universität zu Berlin, 117–120.

Leykum, Hannah & Moosmüller, Sylvia (2019) Phonotaktische und morphonotaktische Konsonantencluster in wortmedialer Position in der österreichischen Standardaussprache (Phonotactic and morphonotactic consonant clusters in word-medial position in Standard Austrian German). In: Bülow, Lars; Fischer, Ann K. & Herbert, Kristina (eds) *Dimensions of Linguistic Space: Variation - Multilingualism - Conceptualisations = Dimensionen des sprachlichen Raums: Variation – Mehrsprachigkeit – Konzeptualisierung*. Berlin: Peter Lang, 127–145. doi:10.3726/b15250/16

Moosmüller, Sylvia (1991) *Hochsprache und Dialekt in Österreich. Soziophonologische Untersuchungen zu ihrer Abgrenzung in Wien, Graz, Salzburg und Innsbruck* (Standard and dialect in Austria. Sociophonetic investigation on their distinction in Vienna, Graz, Salzburg and Innsbruck). [Sprachwissenschaftliche Reihe 1]. Wien: Böhlau.

Myers, James (1995) *The categorical and gradient phonology of variable t-deletion in*

English. International Workshop on Language Variation and Linguistic, Nijmegen.

Nakamura, Mitsuhiro (2015) Conditioning factors in word-final coronal stop deletion in British English: An articulatory-acoustic analysis. In: Leemann, Adrian; Kolly, Marie-José; Schmid, Stephan & Dellwo, Volker (eds) *Trends in Phonetics and Phonology. Studies from German-speaking Europe*. Bern: Peter Lang Ltd, 241–254.

Neu, Helene (1980) Ranking of constraints on /t, d/ deletion in American English: a statistical analysis. In: Labov, William (ed.) *Locating Language in Time and Space*. [Quantitative analyses of linguistic structure 1]. New York: Academic Press, 37–54.

Noll, Anton; White, Jonathan; Balazs, Peter & Deutsch, Werner (2007) *STx - Intelligent Sound Processing, Programmer's Reference*. < https://www.kfs.oeaw.ac.at/stx>.

Plag, Ingo (2014) Phonological and phonetic variability in complex words: An uncharted territory, *Rivista di Linguistica* 26(2), 209–228.

Pluymaekers, Mark; Ernestus, Mirjam; Baayen, R. Harald & Booij, Geert (2010) Morphological effects on fine phonetic detail: The case of Dutch -igheid. In: Fougeron, Cécile; Kühnert, Barbara; D'Imperio, Mariapaola & Vallée, Nathalie (eds) *Laboratory Phonology 10*. [Phonology and phonetics 4-4]. Berlin/New York: De Gruyter Mouton, 511–532. doi:10.1515/9783110224917.5.511

Quasthoff, Uwe; Goldhahn, Dirk & Heyer, Gerhard (2013) *Technical Report Series on Corpus Building. Vol. 1. Deutscher Wortschatz 2012* (2013) <http://asvdoku.informatik.uni-leipzig.de/corpora/data/uploads/corpus-building-vol1-wortschatz-2012.pdf>.

R Core Team (2015) *R: A Language and Environment for Statistical Computing*. R Foundation for Statistical Computing, Vienna. <https://www.R-project.org>.

Schuppler, Barbara; van Dommelen, Wim; Koreman, Jacques & Ernestus, Mirjam (2012) How linguistic and probabilistic properties of a word affect the realization of its final /t/: Studies at the phonemic and subphonemic level, *Journal of Phonetics* 40(4), 595–607. doi:10.1016/j.wocn.2012.05.004

Seyfarth, Scott J. (2016) *Contextual and Morphological Effects in Speech Production*. PhD dissertation, University of California.

Tagliamonte, Sali & Temple, Rosalind (2005) New perspectives on an ol' variable: (t,d) in British English, *Language Variation and Change* 17(03), 281–302. doi:10.1017/S0954394505050118

Zimmerer, Frank; Scharinger, Mathias & Reetz, Henning (2011) When BEAT becomes HOUSE. Factors of word final /t/-deletion in German, *Speech Communication* 53(6), 941–954. doi:10.1016/j.specom.2011.03.006

Zimmerer, Frank; Scharinger, Mathias & Reetz, Henning (2014) Phonological and morphological constraints on German /t/-deletions, *Journal of Phonetics* 45, 64–75. doi:10.1016/j.wocn.2014.03.006

Zydorowicz, Paulina (2007) Polish morphonotactics in first language acquisition, *Wiener Linguistische Gazette* 74, 24–44.

III. The acquisition and processing of (mor)phonotactic consonant clusters in German

SABINE SOMMER-LOLEI[1,2]
KATHARINA KORECKY-KRÖLL[3]
MARKUS CHRISTINER[4]
WOLFGANG U. DRESSLER[1]

1. INTRODUCTION

The aims of this psycholinguistic contribution are to show how morphonotactic and phonotactic German consonant clusters differ 1) in early spontaneous first language acquisition and 2) (more importantly) in processing experiments, under which conditions one of the two cluster types is acquired earlier and processed more accurately and with shorter latency, as well as what the impact of frequency, familiarity and foreignness on the processing of simple words, compounds and morphological derivatives is.

Phonotactics and morphotactics interact in the area of morphonotactics (Dressler & Dziubalska-Kołaczyk 2006). As will be shown in the following sections of this chapter, consonant clusters with and without morpheme boundaries are a good testing ground for the investigation of morphonotactics. Whereas phonotactic consonant clusters are found in simple word stems (e.g. German *Wicht* 'wight'), morphonotactic clusters cross morpheme boundaries in inflected, derived or compound words (e.g. German *(er/sie/es) mach-t* '(s/he/it) makes', *Reich-tum* 'richness', *Pech+tag* 'off-day'). Sometimes morphonotactic clusters are entirely new consonant clusters that can only be found in morphologically complex words (e.g. German *ruf-st* '(you) call'), but sometimes they may also be homophonous with existing phonotactic clusters (e.g. German morphonotactic *lob-st* '(you) praise' vs. phonotactic *Obst* 'fruit'). The question that arises is whether the interaction between phonotactics and morphonotactics facilitates the processing and acquisition of morpho-

---

[1] Austrian Centre for Digital Humanities and Cultural Heritage (ACDH-CH) of the Austrian Academy of Sciences, Vienna & University of Vienna.

[2] Recipient of a DOC-team fellowship of the Austrian Academy of Sciences.

[3] Department of German Studies of the University of Vienna.

[4] Centre for Systematic Musicology, University of Graz & Jāzeps Vītols Latvian Academy of Music.

notactic clusters or makes it more difficult, or if it makes no difference whether a word contains a phonotactic or morphonotactic cluster. In contrast to Slavic languages, German has only very few examples of morphonotactic clusters which arise through vowel deletion, and all clusters involved are homophonous with phonotactic clusters, e.g. in the adjective *risk-ant* 'risky' derived from the noun *Risiko* 'risk'. For a corpus linguistic description of complex German consonant clusters, see Dressler and Kononenko in this volume.

Previous research (Zydorowicz 2007, 2009, 2010; Kamandulytė 2006; Freiberger 2007, 2014; Korecky-Kröll & Dressler 2015; Zydorowicz et al. 2015) has shown no greater acquisitional difficulties for morphonotactic clusters compared to phonotactic clusters in typically developing children. Evidence for the facilitation of acquiring morphonotactic clusters has been found for Polish and Lithuanian, but not for German. Evidence for the ease of processing of German has been divergent (Korecky-Kröll et al. 2014; Celata et al. 2015; Freiberger et al. 2015).

The results of the above investigations have led to the hypothesis (Zydorowicz et al. 2015) that processing ease correlates with the morphological richness of the respective language. Morphological richness is defined as the amount of productive morphology (Dressler 1999, 2004), and it has been demonstrated by Xanthos et al. (2011) that its presence in child-directed speech supports children in developing and speeding up the acquisition of morphology. For processing, our corresponding claim refers to Libben's (2014) principle of maximum opportunity.

German morphology is relatively poor in inflection, which probably explains why we have found no facilitation of the acquisition and processing of morphonotactic clusters, but it is rich in compounding and several areas of derivational morphology.

We examined the influence of (mor)phonotactics in visual word recognition in lexical access and word identification (Korecky-Kröll et al. 2014; Freiberger et al. 2015; Korecky-Kröll et al. 2016; Sommer-Lolei, Korecky-Kröll & Dressler 2017) in order to test the Strong Morphonotactic Hypothesis (Dressler & Dziubalska-Kołaczyk 2006), which claims that morphonotactic consonant clusters facilitate processing and acquisition and lead to higher accuracy because of the significant morphological information those clusters carry. We will test this hypothesis for German, to see whether it will be supported because morphonotactics facilitates word recognition in lexical processing. Or will processing rather be impeded due to the higher processing cost of inflected word forms vs. base forms? Furthermore, we hypothesize first that the Strong Morphonotactic

Hypothesis may not be equally true for all languages and may depend on the morphological richness of a language or its respective morphological subsystem; second, that factors other than the often-overestimated frequency may play a major role in processing.

2. CONSONANT CLUSTERS IN FIRST LANGUAGE ACQUISITION

Freiberger (2014) investigated the early acquisition of morphonotactic and phonotactic consonant clusters in three typically developing monolingual toddlers (1 boy, 2 girls) from high SES backgrounds (HSES), who were acquiring Standard Austrian German. They were recorded longitudinally at their homes in Vienna, from 1 year 7 months (1;7) up to 3;0 years. She divided this period into three[5] developmental phases (phase 1: 1;7–2;0, phase 2: 2;1–2;6, phase 3: 2;7–3;0). All of these data were transcribed and coded by using an adapted German version of CHILDES (cf. MacWhinney 2000). Freiberger analysed 180 minutes per child and phase and investigated all correctly and incorrectly produced consonant clusters in the spontaneous speech of these mother-child interactions in word-initial, -medial and -final position.

The results show, as expected, that all children make significant progress from the first to the third phase, and that the children have more difficulty with word-initial clusters, which are all phonotactic in German, than with word-final clusters. This can be attributed to the fact that final elements are perceived best, well known as the *recency effect* (cf. Eysenck & Keane 2000). In this study no significant morpheme boundary effect was found, which reveals that there is no difference between morphonotactic and phonotactic consonant clusters in the early acquisition of German.

In another investigation by Korecky-Kröll et al. (2016) the spontaneous speech of parent-child interactions of 29 typically developing monolingual and Standard Austrian German-acquiring children from different SES backgrounds (HSES vs. lower SES (LSES)) (7 boys and 8 girls of HSES, 8 boys and 6 girls of LSES) of the INPUT project[6] was analysed. The children were video and audio recorded in everyday situations with their main caretakers in their homes in Vienna at four data points at the

[5] Except for the boy, whose audio recordings already started at age 1;3, and therefore have an additional fourth phase (phase 0: 1;3–1;6), cf. (Freiberger 2014: 7).

[6] INPUT project: 'Investigating Parental and Other Caretakers' Utterances to Kindergarten Children' (SSH11-027) funded by the Wiener Wissenschafts-, Forschungs- und Technologiefonds (WWTF Vienna Science and Technology Fund).

mean ages 3;1, 3;4, 4;4 and 4;8. The most interactive 30 minutes per recording were transcribed, coded and analysed, which is equivalent to 58 hours of spontaneous speech material. The correct use of Cst (consonant +st) clusters, in a medial and final position was examined, in correlation to the effects of the data point, SES and morpheme boundary.

The results demonstrated that the children made significant progress from the third to the fourth data point and also showed a significant effect of the socio-economic status, since LSES children showed lower accuracy. Similarly to Freiberger's investigation (see above), there was no significant influence from the morpheme boundary.

The overall results show that there are no differences in first language acquisition of German between morphonotactic and phonotactic consonant clusters, neither in very young (Freiberger 2014) nor in older children (Korecky-Kröll et al. 2016). This is similar to the findings of Kirk and Demuth (2005) for English, which is a still more weakly inflecting language than German, and unlike the results presented in studies of strong inflecting, morphologically richer languages, such as Polish and Lithuanian (cf. Zydorowicz 2007, 2009, 2010; Kamandulytė 2006; Zydorowicz et al. 2015), in which the authors showed some differences in favour of morphonotactic clusters. This difference might be due to the fact that most of the investigated German morphonotactic clusters occurred in inflected word forms. Still, Freiberger (2007: 20) demonstrated that the presence of a morpheme boundary does not render word recognition and production in child speech (CS) more difficult.

There are two open issues which we would like to address. First, whether or not the preference for morphonotactic clusters in certain languages or their morphological subsystems depends on the degree of morphological richness; and second, whether the acquisition of distinct consonant patterns truly correlates with the presence of a morpheme boundary, or whether, instead, the morpheme boundary itself is the important factor, regardless of the existence of a consonant cluster.

3. CONSONANT CLUSTERS IN PROCESSING

3.1. PREVIOUS EXPERIMENTS

To test the Strong Morphonotactic Hypothesis for German in adult and adolescent processing, four experiments were performed, which led to divergent results. A study by Korecky-Kröll et al. (2014) used a visual sequence targeting experiment in which 84 native Standard Austrian German-speaking participants had to detect whether a given stimulus contained either one letter (T) or a sequence of two letters (ST, AN). The experiment was divided into four different tasks: find T (in words containing ST); find T (in a word containing only T, but not ST); find ST; and find AN. In the first two parts participants had to find T a) in a consonant+st (Cst) sequence (e.g. *Obst* 'fruit' vs. *lob-st* 'you praise') and b) in a consonant+t (Ct) combination (e.g. *Karton* 'cardboard' vs. *dankte* 'thanked', *Lift* 'elevator' vs. *pack-t* '(s/he/it) packs'). In the third task, participants had to detect ST in a word presented visually (e.g. *Stempel* 'stamp' vs. *brav-ste* (good-SUP) 'best' superlative); and in the fourth, they had to find AN (e.g. *Fasan* 'pheasant' vs. *vor-an* 'ahead'). Half of the stimuli did not contain the respective sequence, whereas the other half was divided into subgroups that contained the sequence in different positions. For example, in the find T (in T) experiment, 96 stimuli did not contain a /t/, whereas 16 stimuli contained a /t/ in the initial position, 16 in a medial position without morpheme boundary, 16 in a medial position with morpheme boundary, 16 in the final position without morpheme boundary, 16 in the final position with morpheme boundary as a default and 16 in the final position with obligatory morpheme boundary (after a diphthong or long vowel).

Besides other factors, the authors reported a significant facilitating impact from the morpheme boundary only in terms of reaction times (RT), but not of accuracy (ACC), which indicates processing on a sublexical level.

Celata et al. (2015) examined the processing of morphonotactic and phonotactic clusters in German in two different experiments. First, they performed a split cluster task, in which 38 adults (29 years and older) and 26 adolescents (11 to 15 years of age), all native speakers of Standard Austrian German, had to create novel diminutives and attenuative forms by inserting the vowel /i/ between two consonants (CC→CiC). They were presented with 14 monosyllabic test items ending in a Cst-cluster, half containing a morphonotactic cluster, half a phonotactic one, and 56 filler words with differing clusters. Thus, they had to transform, for example, a Cst-cluster /nst/ into /nist/ or /nsit/ in phonotactic *Dunst* 'mist' (→ **Dunist* or **Dunsit*) and in morphonotactic *kenn-st* 'you know' (→ **kennist* or **kennsit*). The result showed an overall preference for /ist/ over /sit/ responses and, only within the adult group, high accuracies regardless of the type of cluster. For the group of adolescents, the morphonotactic clusters were significantly easier to split than the phonotactic ones, whereas the adult group only showed a trend in favour of the stimuli containing a morpheme boundary. This demonstrates that the presence of a morpheme boundary tends to be helpful in connection with a word modifying task.

Second, a fragment monitoring task was conducted with 28 adolescents (aged 12 to 16) and 41 adults (aged 25 to 59), again all native speakers of Standard Austrian German. Participants were visually presented with a string in capital letters in the centre of the screen, while hearing words over headphones. They had to decide as quickly as possible whether the auditorily perceived word contained the string presented on the screen. In this experiment 30 German words, with a Cst-cluster in the mid- or final position, and 75 filler words, containing other clusters, served as stimuli (e.g. the Cst-cluster /nst/ in phonotactic *Kunst* 'art' vs. morphonotactic *kenn-st* 'you know').

The results showed that, overall, adults were significantly more accurate compared to the group of adolescents, which shows again that the acquisition of phonology and morphonology is not completely finished in adolescence. Despite our expectations, the presence of a morpheme boundary had no effect on adult accuracy, although it did have an effect in the latency of the younger group, with phonotactic patterns being detected faster than morphonotactic ones. Also, the adolescents made more errors in morphonotactic items. The authors point to the significant impact of frequency in this case, since high-frequency items were more often not only judged correctly, but also faster than low-frequency ones in the adult group, whereas this frequency difference did not show as much of an effect in adolescents. This points to different processing strategies in such a recognition task across ages.

Since the above experiments focused only on the sublexical level, as either morphemes, parts of morphemes or clusters that contained morphemes were processed, there was a strong need to investigate adult language processing on a higher level of language awareness, namely the lexical level.

3.2. Experiments on lexical access

In order to investigate the influence of (mor)phonotactics in lexical processing and to see whether morphonotactics facilitates or impedes visual word recognition, various experiments were performed within our research project.

The findings of all new experiments are first summarized and only afterwards are they accurately described. To investigate the processing of morphonotactic and phonotactic consonant clusters in whole word recognition, we conducted a progressive demasking task (PDT) and four different lexical decision tasks (LDT):

1. Inflection vs. simplex words (LDT 1)
2. Progressive demasking task on inflection vs. simplex words (PDT)
3. Compounds vs. simplex nouns (LDT 2)
4. Derivations vs. simplex nouns (LDT 3)
5. Compounds and derivations vs. simplex nouns (LDT 4)

Previous studies on whole-word processing have demonstrated a higher processing cost for inflected word forms as opposed to monomorphemic words (e.g. Finnish, cf. Laine et al. 1999) or for inflected base forms (e.g. German, cf. Günther 1988). Therefore, the first experiments (LDT 1 and PDT) were created by Freiberger et al. (2015) to test whether native speakers of German show similar tendencies and whether they are sensitive to the presence of a morpheme boundary within a consonant cluster (e.g. /gt/, /bl/, /mt/) when the item is an inflectional form, or whether the morpheme boundary would not delay processing.

Both experiments (LDT 1 and PDT) contained inflected word forms which are non-citation forms. This suggested that it might be problematic to compare a citation form to a non-citation form. Therefore, Korecky-Kröll et al. (2016) performed another lexical decision task (LDT 2) in order to clarify this issue. Instead of comparing the processing of inflectional forms to monomorphemic words, compounds, which are citation forms like monomorphemic words, were used. Compounding is also a morphologically rich domain of German, richer than inflection, which is another issue that needed to be addressed. We hypothesized that compounds would be processed not only more accurately but also much faster than monomorphemic words.

In order to cover all categories of word formation, Sommer-Lolei et al. (2017) also conducted an experiment with derived words compared to monomorphemic words (LDT 3). Derivations, like compounds, are citation forms, but are expected to be harder to process, because compounds are morphosemantically more transparent than comparable derivations.

In our final lexical decision task 4 we combined the two previous experiments (LDT 2 and 3) into one, considering two newly introduced variables, namely familiarity and foreignness (see also 3.7).

3.3. Methodology

To investigate lexical access, four lexical decision tasks were performed. The experiments (LDT 1, 2 and 3) were designed using the behavioural research software E-Prime 3.0 (Psychology Software Tools, Pittsburgh, PA) and were all carried out on the same Windows laptop (Freiberger et al. 2015; Korecky-Kröll et al. 2016; Sommer-Lolei et al. 2017). LDT 4 was an online experiment, programmed and provided by URL: https://quest.christiner.at/. Due to the high number of participants that were all tested in one day, we tested on several Windows computers simultaneously. All of the test items were presented to the participants visually, capitalized in the centre of the screen, following a fixation cross. Participants had to decide as accurately and quickly as possible whether the presented string was an existing German word or not. The relevant keys were marked with a green sticker for an affirmative response, and a red sticker for a negative response. All reaction times measured in LDT 1, 2 and 3 that were below 300 ms or exceeded 2500 ms were excluded from the analysis. For LDT 4 reaction times were measured but considered as not reliable due to the high number of different computers used at the same time and intermittent connectivity issues.

The progressive demasking task (PDT) was used to test word identification. The experiment was designed using the PDT software (Dufau, Stevens & Grainger 2008). The cut-off values in this experiment were < 300 ms and > 3500 ms. Participants had to identify on their computer screen a slowly demasking stimulus and to confirm identification of it as soon as possible by pressing a key. As a result, the word disappeared from the screen and they had to type the previously identified word as quickly as possible. The same Windows laptop was used to conduct the experiment as in LDT 1, 2 and 3.

The choice of stimuli for LDT 4 was established as a consequence of two ratings that revealed the degree of familiarity and foreignness of the test items previously used in LDT 2 and 3. In the first rating of compounds vs. monomorphemic words, participants got a list of 96 items and had to decide whether or not the word on the list was a foreign word, and they had to judge spontaneously how familiar they are with this word. While the foreignness rating was a decision task (Yes or No), the familiarity rating had a range on a scale from 1 (well known) up to 5 (unknown). This was conducted using an interactive PDF (Adobe Acrobat DC). Each rating was either forwarded immediately to the investigator via email or all ratings filled in by hand on a printed form were handed in by the participants.

The second rating of derivations vs. monomorphemic words used an online questionnaire, programmed and provided by Markus Christiner on an online platform, URL: https://quest.christiner.at/. Similarly to the first rating, participants had to decide on the foreignness and familiarity of 96 stimulus words that were presented one after the other, whenever the participant clicked on the *Weiter* 'next/go on' button. It was not possible to measure reaction times.

3.4. Materials

In each of the tasks the experimental items were 96 German words and 96 German-based non-words (one letter of a German word was changed in the monomorphemic words, two letters were changed in the compound and derivation-based items, i.e. one consonant or vowel in each of the two morphological parts), with the exception of LDT 4, in which the stimuli were 96 German words and 32 German-based non-words, divided into four conditions, as presented in Table 1:

Table 1. Conditions of the test stimuli

Condition		**Explanation**
1	M+P+	containing a consonant cluster that crosses the morpheme boundary
2	M+P–	containing a morpheme boundary, but no consonant cluster
3	M–P+	monomorphemic word containing a consonant cluster
4	M–P–	monomorphemic word without a consonant cluster

This results in 24 words and 24 non-words per condition. Half of the items contained a morpheme boundary, while the other half did not, which is exactly the same as the items containing or not containing a consonant cluster. In LDT 1 and the PDT (Freiberger et al. 2015), stimulus words contained only biconsonantal clusters (e.g. /gr/, /br/), whereas in LDT 2 (Korecky-Kröll et al. 2016), LDT 3 (Sommer-Lolei et al. 2017) and LDT 4, bi- and triconsonantal clusters occurred (e.g. /rtn/, /lst/). The position of the consonant clusters was either in the final (LDT 1) or in a medial position (LDT 2, 3 and 4). For every morphonotactic consonant cluster there existed a phonotactic match (e.g. LDT 2 on compounds: (M+P+) *Haus+tier* 'domestic animal' vs. (M–P+) *Kastanie* 'chestnut'). Therefore, we also matched conditions 2 and 4 (e.g. LDT 3 on derivations: (M+P–) *Zeig-er* 'pointer' vs. (M–P–) *Lager* 'storage'). Examples of stimuli for each experiment are listed in Table 2; for a summarizing overview of the tasks, see Tables 3 and 4. All of the items were balanced for word length, syllables and average word frequency (taken as the number of occurrences from the CELEX, the Austrian Media Corpus (AMC[7]) and also the *Leipzig Deutscher Wortschatz Online* databases).

Table 2. Examples for German words used in the experiments per condition

Task	LDT 1 & PDT (Inflection)	LDT 2 (Compounding)	LDT 3 (Derivation)
		LDT 4 (Compounding and Derivation)	
Cond. 1 (M+P+)	*wag-te* 'dared'	*Haus+tier* 'domestic animal'	*Eitel-keit* 'vanity'
triconsonantal clusters	-	*Hals+tuch* 'scarf'	*Gärt-ner* 'gardener'
Cond. 2 (M+P–)	*heb-en* 'lift'	*Tee+tasse* 'teacup'	*Zeig-er* 'pointer'
Cond. 3 (M–P+)	*Zimt* 'cinnamon'	*Kastanie* 'chestnut'	*Balsam* 'balm'
triconsonantal clusters	-	*Holster* 'holster'	*Partner* 'partner'
Cond. 4 (M–P–)	*Mücke* 'mosquito'	*Rakete* 'rocket'	*Lager* 'storage'

3.5. Participants

All the participants were adult monolingual native speakers of Standard Austrian German. None of them reported visual or neurological impairments or a history of language disorders.

In LDT 1, in which processing of inflectional forms was compared to monomorphemic word processing, 46 adults (aged 19 to 35) participated.

In the progressive demasking task, in which the same inflectional forms and monomorphemic words taken from the previously conducted LDT 1 had to be identified, 45 adults (aged 19 to 31) participated, likewise in LDT 2, in which the processing of monomorphemic words was compared to the processing of compounds and in LDT 3, where the processing of derivations compared to monomorphemic words was investigated.

The first rating of foreignness and familiarity with regard to the list of compounds and monomorphemic words was conducted with 130 adult participants (aged 18 to 51); the second rating of the stimulus word list

[7] The Austrian Media Corpus of the Austrian Academy of Sciences, based on APA (Austrian Press Agency) data, consists of over 10 billion word tokens. URL: https://www.oeaw.ac.at/acdh/tools/amc-austria-media-corpus/ [20.03.2019].

of derivations and monomorphemic words was performed by 102 adults (aged 20 to 59). Both ratings were used for stimulus word selection in LDT 4.

In LDT 4, as our most recently performed experiment, in which 84 adults (aged 18 to 36) participated, we united the previous two experiments LDT 2 and 3 in order to investigate the processing of compounds and derivations compared to monomorphemic words, in consideration of the familiarity and foreignness ratings of the stimulus words, where we selected in equal parts very familiar, familiar, very unfamiliar, very foreign, foreign and non-foreign stimulus words (compounds, derivations and monomorphemic nouns).

For a summary of all the performed tasks, ratings and participants, see Tables 3, 4 and 5:

Table 3. Overview of the visual word recognition tasks on inflection

Task	**LDT 1**	**PDT**
	Inflection	Inflection
No. participants (age)	46 (19–35 yrs.)	45 (19–31 yrs.)
Method	E-Prime 3.0	PDT Software
Computer	Win. Laptop	Win. Laptop
RTs measured	Yes	Yes
Cut off values ms	< 300 > 2500	< 300 > 3500
No. stimulus words	96	96
No. stimulus non-words	96	96
Conditions (Tables 1, 2)	1–4	1–4

Table 4. Overview of the lexical decision tasks on compounding and derivation

Task	**LDT 2**	**LDT 3**	**LDT 4**
	Compounding	Derivation	Comp. & Derivation
No. participants (age)	45 (19–31 yrs.)	45 (19–31 yrs.)	84 (18–51yrs.)
Method	E-Prime 3.0	E-Prime 3.0	Online
Computer	Win. Laptop	Win. Laptop	Various Computers
RTs measured	Yes	Yes	Yes
Cut off values ms	< 300 > 2500	< 300 > 2500	RT not reliable
No. stimulus words	96	96	96
No. stimulus non-words	96	96	32
Conditions (Tables 1, 2)	1–4	1–4	1–4

Table 5. Overview of the familiarity and foreignness ratings

	Rating 1	Rating 2
	Comp. and simplex words	Deriv. and simplex words
No. stimuli	96	96
No. participants (age)	130 (18–51 yrs.)	102 (20–59 yrs.)
Method	interactive PDF (Adobe Acrobat DC)	Online questionnaire
Familiarity (scalar)	1 (well known) to 5 (unknown)	
Foreignness (nominal)	Yes *or* No	

3.6. Results of the processing experiments

In the first whole-word recognition tasks, conducted by Freiberger et al. (2015), divergent results were found. Regarding the LDT 1 and the PDT on inflection, they found that in both experiments words with a morpheme boundary were significantly more difficult to process than all the other categories. In particular, the category M+P+, which are strings that contain a morpheme boundary and a consonant cluster, showed the highest latency, and in the lexical decision task also the lowest accuracy. This is in accordance with processing models which assume that affixed words are decomposed into base form and affix, which leads to higher processing costs. They did not find this accuracy result in the PDT; instead words without a morpheme boundary and with a consonant cluster (M–P+) were processed more accurately. The longer reaction times for the M+P+ items can be explained by the fact that these strings were all inflectional forms. Therefore, Freiberger and colleagues concluded that it is problematic to compare a non-citation form with a citation form, as already mentioned above, but also, this may be due to the fact that German is only a weakly inflecting language, in which inflectional morphology is not important enough to facilitate lexical processing. In the strongly inflecting language Polish, Zydorowicz and Dziubalska-Kołaczyk (2017) found that the morpheme boundary helped processing. The results furthermore show that it is not the cluster that renders word recognition more difficult, but rather the morpheme boundary combined with the cluster. In this case the Strong Morphonotactic Hypothesis could not be confirmed for German, although there had been some evidence for it on the sublexical level in previous experiments (see 3.1).

In order to verify these findings and to test the hypothesis concerning the impact of citation forms, Korecky-Kröll et al. (2016) conducted the second experiment, LDT 2, on compounding. Since inflected word forms were included in the first experiments (Freiberger et al. 2015, see above), we wanted to see whether words that are citation forms, like monomorphemic words, and that derive from a morphologically rich domain of German, much richer than inflection, would lead the participants to a different behaviour. The results for accuracy showed that compounds with morphonotactic clusters (M+P+ items, with morpheme boundary and consonant cluster), but also M+P– items (compounds without a consonant cluster) show significantly higher accuracy than either type of monomorphemic words. This diverges from the results of the previous lexical decision experiments on inflection, and therefore supports the Strong Morphonotactic Hypothesis. The results for latency showed no significant difference, but a trend in favour of M+P+ compounds (with morpheme boundary and with consonant cluster).

These results have demonstrated that the decomposition of compounds does not slow down processing but is, rather, automatic, which supports Libben's (2014) principle of maximum opportunity.

Korecky-Kröll et al. (2016) therefore concluded that the facilitation process in the acquisition and processing of morphonotactic clusters only seems to apply in a language or linguistic domain that is morphologically rich, and it was suggested that the Strong Morphonotactic Hypothesis be modified accordingly (also in Sommer-Lolei et al. 2017). Thus, the interaction with morphology appears to facilitate processing where it "is worth it".

The third lexical decision experiment on derivational morphology (LDT 3) was performed by Sommer-Lolei et al. (2017) in order to support our theoretical claim that the morphological richness of a certain area facilitates processing, i.e. by also investigating the derivational domain.

The results of the LDT 3 demonstrated that M+P– items in particular (derivations containing a morpheme boundary, but no consonant cluster), but also M+P+ items (derivations containing a morpheme boundary and a consonant cluster), yield a significantly higher accuracy and are processed significantly faster than both types of monomorphemic words. Derived nouns (derived via productive word-formation rules) were processed more accurately than simplex nouns. Unlike the previous experiment on compounding (Korecky-Kröll et al. 2016, see above), these results do not support the Strong Morphonotactic Hypothesis directly but only indirectly, insofar as we found a positive effect on processing whenever a morpheme boundary is present.

To demonstrate differences in the processing of morphonotactic and phonotactic consonant clusters in compounds, derivations and monomorphemic words (LDT 4), a repeated measures ANOVA was performed on the mean values of the correct responses. The results show, with a Greenhouse-Geisser correction, that words containing a morpheme boundary were processed significantly differently $F(2.48,195.73) = 30.76, p < 0.01$, regardless of whether the string contained a consonant cluster or not. Condition 1 (M+P+ Mean = 0.85) was significantly different from conditions 3 (M–P+ Mean = 0.79) and 4 (M–P– Mean = 0.79) but not from condition 2 (M+P– Mean = 0.84). M+P+ and M+P– items were significantly different from both categories without a morpheme boundary.

3.7. Results of the familiarity and foreignness ratings

In our lexical decision tasks on compounds (LDT 2) and derivations (LDT 3) the high number of foreign words within the group of monomorphemic words (e.g. *Taifun* 'typhoon', *Baklava* 'baklava') that were used within the experiments still seemed problematic to us as a possible confounding factor. Use of these items was due to the necessity of matching compounds and derivations to monomorphemic words in frequency and word length.

Therefore, we had 130 German native speakers rate all our stimulus words for the compound experiment in terms of the degree of familiarity and foreignness, which revealed that the four categories of stimuli differed significantly in their perceived degree of foreignness (see Figure 1), whereas in the familiarity rating only monomorphemic words without consonant clusters (M–P–) were rated significantly less familiar than all other categories (see Figure 2):

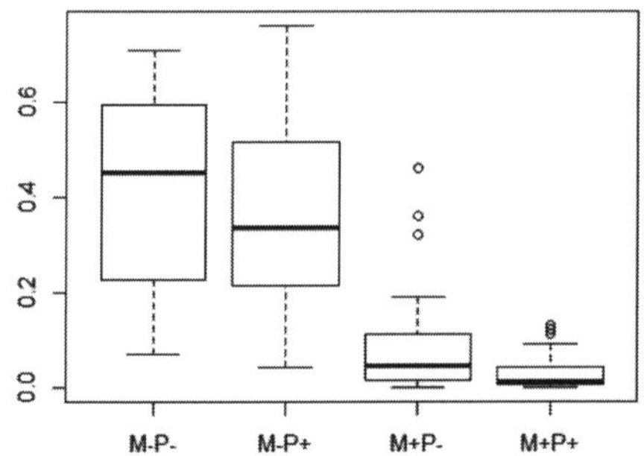

Figure 1. Degree of foreignness in the four categories (Rating of stimulus words for LDT 2)

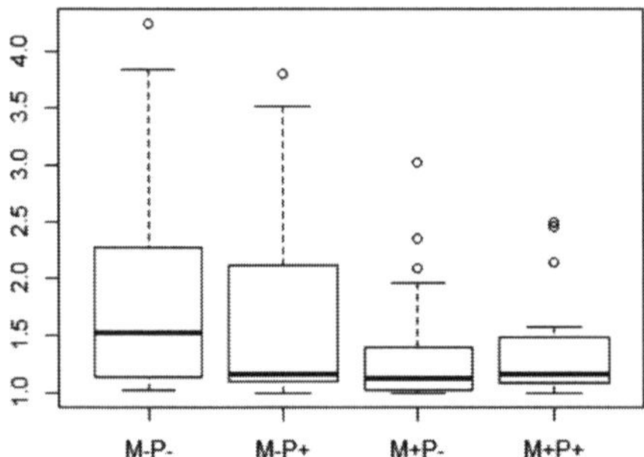

Figure 2. Degree of familiarity in the four categories
(Rating of stimulus words for LDT 2)

The results for compounds and monomorphemic words show that foreignness and, especially, unfamiliarity reduce accuracy and delay the speed of processing significantly.

Although familiarity and foreignness were less likely to constitute intervening variables for derivations than for compounds, we nevertheless had the 96 stimulus words rated for this experiment by 102 native speakers of German, which revealed a significant difference between the categories M– and M+ regarding the degree of foreignness (see Figure 3). In the familiarity rating we found no significant difference between the four categories (see Figure 4).

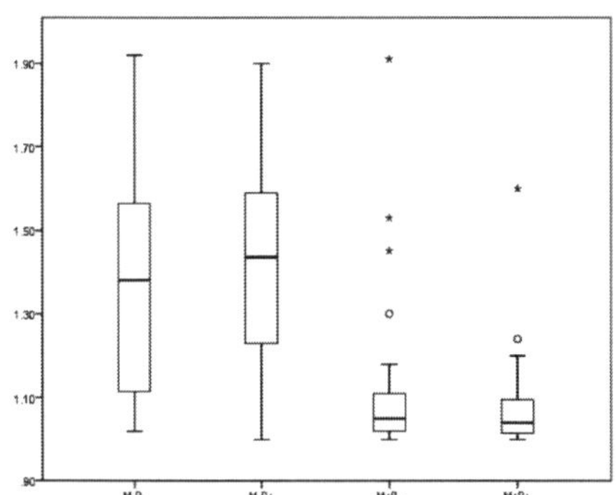

Figure 3. Degree of foreignness in the four categories
(Rating of stimulus words for LDT 3)

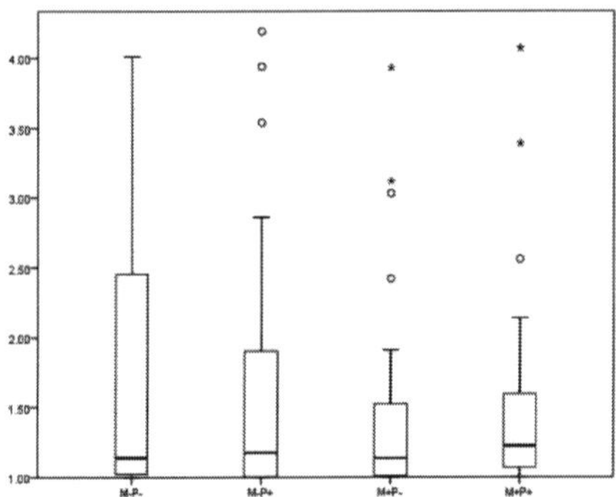

Figure 4. Degree of familiarity in the four categories
(Rating of stimulus words for LDT 3)

4. STATISTICAL ANALYSES

4.1. IMPACT OF FREQUENCY, FAMILIARITY AND FOREIGNNESS ON ACCURACY

As mentioned above, we hypothesized that familiar words, ranked in advance by native speakers of Standard Austrian German (see also 3.4), would be processed significantly more accurately than unfamiliar words and second, that stimulus words judged as foreign would result in significantly lower accuracy than all of the other words.

To demonstrate the effects of frequency, familiarity and foreignness in adult language processing we analysed their impact in terms of accuracy of words (non-words were excluded) in LDT 2 (compounds vs. simplex nouns), LDT 3 (derivations vs. simplex nouns) and LDT 4 (compounds and derivations vs. simplex nouns).

As for LDT 2 (Korecky-Kröll et al. 2016), statistical analyses of the accuracy of words reveal that words with a high AMC token frequency are significantly more likely to be judged correctly and that high-frequency words containing a morpheme boundary, especially M+P+ items, are processed significantly more accurately than words without one. In terms of familiarity and foreignness, we found that stimulus words that are either unfamiliar and/or foreign have significantly less accurate results than familiar and non-foreign words. In addition, there is no difference in this respect in the processing of morphonotactic and phonotactic consonant clusters across the four categories.

In our LDT 3 on derivations compared to monomorphemic nouns (Sommer-Lolei et al. 2017), words containing a morpheme boundary have significantly more accurate results compared to monomorphemic words, regardless of the absence or presence of a consonant cluster. Also, we found that words without a consonant cluster and without a morpheme boundary (M–P–) are processed significantly less accurately than M–P+, which demonstrates a processing strategy of preferring a phonotactic consonant cluster whenever no morpheme boundary is present. In other words, the presence of a morpheme boundary leads to significantly higher results than the presence of a cluster. This indicates the relevance of morpheme boundaries.

Similar to our finding in LDT 2, we found, with regard to familiarity and foreignness, that stimulus words that are either unfamiliar or foreign or both have significantly less accurate results than familiar/non-foreign words. In the case of familiarity of items, there is no difference in the processing of morphonotactic and phonotactic consonant clusters. However, when items are foreign, we found that words with a phonotactic consonant cluster (M–P+) are processed significantly more accurately compared to all other categories.

This appears to mean that (rather) foreign words of limited length are expected to be monomorphemic words, and this respects the fact that more simplex words are loaned than affixed words, in contrast to loaned English compounds.

By merging the previously conducted two experiments into one new experiment with respect to the degree of familiarity and of foreignness of the stimulus words, we found, with regard to the impact of token frequency, that words containing a morpheme boundary were processed with significantly greater accuracy compared to monomorphemic words, with M+P– items scoring highest. The processing of unfamiliar or foreign words in LDT 4 shows that these items are processed significantly less accurately, as in the previously conducted LDT 2 and 3. For familiarity we found no significant difference between the four categories. Foreign words containing a morpheme boundary have significantly less accurate results than words without it.

Statistical analyses of accuracy undertaken by means of a repeated measures ANOVA reveal differences in the processing of the three categories (compounds, derivations, simplex nouns). The results show that each of the three categories led to highly significant differences from each other: $F(2,158) = 35.29$, $p < 0.01$. Independently of whether the item was a word or a non-word, compounds were processed with significantly more accuracy than simplex nouns, whereas derived words resulted in an intermediary position, significantly different from both compounds and monomorphemic nouns (see Figure 5).

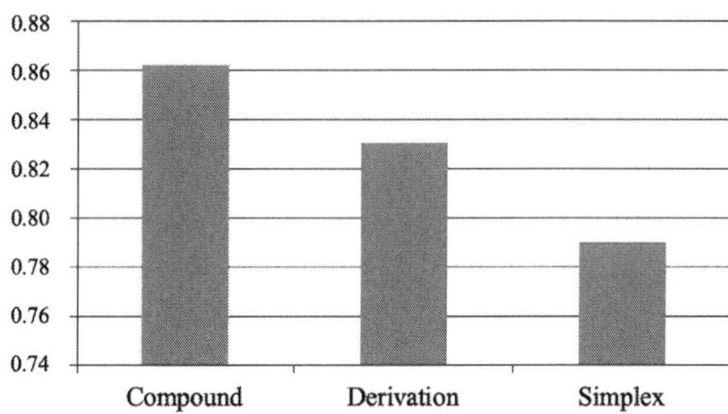

Figure 5. Mean values of accuracy in processing in compounds, derivations and simplex words

When analysing our data (LDT 2, 3 and 4) with regard to familiarity by using general linear mixed-effects models (Bates et al. 2015), we found that very unfamiliar words are processed with significantly less accuracy in all three experiments, but that there were no significant differences with regard to the presence vs. absence of a morpheme boundary or consonant cluster or both. Familiarity is shown to be a highly influential factor when it comes to compounds (LDT 2 and 4), whereas in LDT 3 (derivations vs. simplex nouns), familiarity is an intervening variable to a lesser extent (see Table 6).

It is a novel finding, as first presented by Sommer-Lolei et al. (2017), that familiarity is a more important variable in compounds than foreignness, which itself is more important than token frequency. The results for LDT 2 show that foreignness is much closer to frequency than to familiarity. Therefore, we can conclude that although all three variables are significant in respect of processing, familiarity is the most important factor when dealing with compounds, which is also a warning against relying excessively on frequency. Instead, other variables, in particular familiarity, should be considered as well.

Thus, results point to the fact that it is important whether a given string is a citation form or not, and, additionally, whether the item contains a morpheme boundary is rather important, although we only found effects of morphonotactic consonant clusters in LDT 2 and 4, which demonstrates the strong impact of compounds.

Overall, the presence of a morpheme boundary facilitates word recognition and processing except for unfamiliar and foreign words, regardless of whether there is a consonant cluster or not.

Table 6. Hierarchy of influencing factors on the accuracy of German stimulus words

Accuracy of words in:			
LDT 2 (Comp. vs. Simplex)	**Familiarity** >	*Foreignness* >	Frequency
z values and significance levels[8]	-14.007***	-4.935***	3.781***
AIC values[9]	1906.541	1996.92	2006.647
LDT 3 (Deriv. vs. Simplex)	Frequency >	**Familiarity** >	*Foreignness*
z values and significance levels	12.631***	-14.017***	-5.609***
AIC values	1489.297	1494.002	1576.088
LDT 4 (Comp./Deriv. vs. Simp.)	**Familiarity** >	Frequency >	*Foreignness*
z values and significance levels	-12.573***	8.361***	-5.807***
AIC values	3493.344	3529.927	3559.36

4.2. Influence of frequency, familiarity and foreignness on latency

Reaction times were measured for LDT 2 and 3, but as already mentioned above, this was impossible for LDT 4. The results demonstrate in both experiments that frequency has an impact in the sense that words with a high token frequency in the AMC corpus are processed significantly faster, regardless of whether the word contains a morpheme boundary and/or a consonant cluster or not. Thus, the positive influence of a morpheme boundary on accuracy has no correspondence in latency. Interestingly, the interaction of morphology with phonological processing appears to increase accuracy, because accuracy is monitored on one additional level, whereas it neither slows down nor accelerates processing significantly.

In terms of familiarity, we find that unknown or very unfamiliar words were processed significantly slower in both experiments. In LDT 2 (com-

[8] The following significance levels were selected: * 0.05, ** 0.01, *** 0.001. Please note that the negative z values for the foreignness and familiarity rating are due to the coding. For foreignness, this is more intuitive: if a word was rated as being not a foreign word, this was coded as 1, whereas 2 indicated that it was rated as a foreign word. Therefore, as expected, the accuracy of the participants is higher if the word is less foreign. However, the familiarity rating may appear somewhat counterintuitive as it was, instead, an unfamiliarity rating, ranging from 1 (well known or familiar) to 5 (unknown or unfamiliar). This leads to the negative z values: the participants' accuracy is higher if a word is less unfamiliar (i.e. more familiar).

[9] AIC refers to the Akaike Information Criterion (see e.g. Levshina 2015: 149), which was used as the primary criterion for model selection: the smaller the AIC value, the better the fit of the respective model.

pounds vs. simplex nouns), the analysis of reaction times shows that words containing a morpheme boundary but no consonant cluster (M+P–) delay processing significantly, followed by words with a morpheme boundary and cluster (M+P+), which show a weaker effect on latency. In LDT 3 (derivations), we did not find significant differences of this type.

Regarding the degree of foreignness, the analysis reveals that highly foreign words are processed significantly slower in both experiments which is also the case for stimulus words containing a morpheme boundary (with or without consonant cluster). Analysis of LDT 2 (compounding) shows that words with a morpheme boundary that also contain a consonant cluster (M+P+) delay processing with high significance, followed by words with a morpheme boundary and without a consonant cluster (M+P–), which tend to be processed slightly faster. Interestingly we find the opposite picture when analysing data from our LDT 3, which means that words with a morpheme boundary but without a consonant cluster (M+P–) are processed significantly more slowly than the M+P+ items. This points to the fact that the presence of a morphonotactic consonant cluster delays processing in foreign compounds but only shows a weak effect on the latency of foreign derivatives.

As summarized in Table 7, we conclude that with regard to the latency of compounding, familiarity is the major influencing factor, whereas it is frequency that plays a highly important role when processing derivations.

Table 7. Hierarchy of influencing factors on the latency of German stimulus words

Latency of words in:			
LDT 2 (Comp. vs. Simplex)	**Familiarity** >	*Foreignness* >	Frequency
z values and significance levels	8.577***	4.669***	-4.980***
AIC values	-5732.506	-5701.464	-5700.359
LDT 3 (Deriv. vs. Simplex)	Frequency >	**Familiarity** >	*Foreignness*
z values and significance levels	-12.340***	8.370***	6.313***
AIC values	-6361.651	-6324.792	-6308.46

Morpheme boundaries tended to be helpful on the sublexical level, as found by Celata et al. (2015) in the split cluster task, where frequency also had an important impact (see 3.1). By contrast, our results on lexical processing in terms of latency show significant delays in the presence of morpheme boundaries in unfamiliar and/or foreign words, whereas morpheme boundaries were helpful in familiar and non-foreign words. Frequency was always helpful, but often much less so than familiarity.

5. CONCLUSION

As for German, no effect of the morphonotactic character of consonant clusters is shown in inflection. Therefore, the Strong Morphonotactic Hypothesis is not supported for German inflection, neither in first language acquisition nor in adult or adolescent language processing.

The Strong Morphonotactic Hypothesis could only be supported for German compounding, where the strongest facilitating effect was found for morpheme boundaries with consonant clusters. However, in derivatives too, positive effects of morpheme boundaries (with and without consonant clusters) on processing were found. Nevertheless, when compounds, derivatives and monomorphemic words were directly compared within the same participants, compounds showed significantly higher levels of accuracy than derivatives. This points to the second compound constituent being more readily identifiable, due to its coexistence as an autonomous lexical element, compared to the harder process of retrieving suffixes (inflectional or derivational suffixes). In processing, this is a consequence of the process of chunking elements (here phonemes and graphemes). Apparently morphological chunking is one of the normal processing strategies. Therefore, it is desirable to conduct further experiments in which morpheme and syllable chunking can be compared.

Words are processed faster and significantly more accurately, the more familiar a stimulus word is (particularly in compounding) and, to a lesser extent, the more frequent it is (particularly in derivations). This greater effect of familiarity can be linked to Libben's (2014) principle of opportunity: in compounds, the familiarity of both the whole compound and of the word families of its constituents facilitates processing, whereas the familiarity of the more abstract, i.e. much less morphosemantically descriptive suffixes must have a much smaller influence. As a consequence, the frequency and productivity of suffixes has a relatively greater importance.

ACKNOWLEDGEMENTS

This investigation was performed within the International Cooperation Project 'Human Behaviour and Machine Simulation in the Processing of (Mor)Phonotactics'. We thank the Austrian Science Fund (FWF): [I 1394-G23] for its support.

Sabine Sommer-Lolei is a recipient of a DOC-team fellowship of the Austrian Academy of Sciences. Markus Christiner's investigation is funded within the Post-DocTrack Programme of the OeAW.

We are sincerely grateful to Eva Maria Freiberger who worked as a project collaborator in the first project phase. She designed the LDT 1 and the PDT experiment, collected the data for these experiments and was also involved in their analysis. Furthermore, she did pioneering work on the acquisition of German morphonotactics.

We also want to thank Angelika Wukowits for supervising and executing one of the experiments together with Markus Christiner in the Secondary School for Economic Professions and the Educational Institution for Elementary Pedagogy at Sancta Christiana in Frohsdorf, Austria, with our special thanks to all students who took part in our task and to the director Dr. Alexander Kucera and Mag. Dr. Barbara Bohn for the general organization of the Science Day.

REFERENCES

Bates, Douglas; Mächler, Martin; Bolker, Ben & Walker, Steve (2015) Fitting linear mixed-effects models using lme4, *Journal of Statistical Software* 67(1), 1–48.

Celata, Chiara; Korecky-Kröll, Katharina; Ricci, Irene & Dressler, Wolfgang U. (2015) Phonotactic processing and morpheme boundaries: word-final /Cst/ clusters in German, *Italian Journal of Linguistics* 27(1), 85–110.

Dressler, Wolfgang U. (1999) Ricchezza e Complessità Morfologica (Morphological Richness and Complexity). In: SLI Società di Linguistica Italiana, *Fonologia e Morfologia dell'Italiano e dei Dialetti d'Italia. Atti del 21. Congresso SLI.* Roma: Bulzoni, 587–597.

Dressler, Wolfgang U. (2004) Degrees of grammatical productivity in inflectional morphology, *Italian Journal of Linguistics* 15, 31–62.

Dressler, Wolfgang U. & Dziubalska-Kołaczyk, Katarzyna (2006) Proposing morphonotactics, *Italian Journal of Linguistics* 18(2), 249–266.

Dufau, Stéphane; Stevens, Michaël & Grainger, Jonathan (2008) Windows executable software for the progressive demasking task, *Behavior Research Methods* 40(1), 33–37.

Eysenck, Michael W. & Keane, Mark T. (2000) *Cognitive Psychology. A Student's Handbook.* East Sussex: Psychology Press.

Freiberger, Eva M. (2007) Morphonotaktik im Erstspracherwerb des Deutschen (Morphonotactics in first language acquisition of German), *Wiener Linguistische Gazette* 74, 1–23.

Freiberger, Eva M. (2014) Der Erwerb von Konsonantenclustern im Deutschen: eine Untersuchung longitudinaler Spontansprachkorpora (The acquisition of consonant clusters in German: an investigation of longitudinal spontaneous speech corpora), *Slowakische Zeitschrift für Germanistik* 6(2), 5–23.

Freiberger, Eva M.; Korecky-Kröll, Katharina; Calderone, Basilio & Dressler, Wolfgang U. (2015) Morpheme boundaries inside consonant clusters delay visual word recognition: Evidence from a lexical decision and a progressive demasking experiment. 3rd International Workshop on Phonotactics and Phonotactic Modeling (PPM 2015). Vienna, 26 November 2015.

Günther, Hartmut (1988) Oblique word forms in visual word recognition, *Linguistics* 26, 583–600.

Kamandulytė, Laura (2006) The acquisition of morphonotactics in Lithuanian, *Wiener Linguistische Gazette* 73, 88–96.

Kirk, Cecilia & Demuth, Katherine (2005) Asymmetries in the acquisition of word-initial and word-final consonant clusters, *Journal of Child Language* 32, 709–734. doi:10.1017/S0305000905007130

Korecky-Kröll, Katharina & Dressler, Wolfgang U. (2015) (Mor)phonotactics in high vs. low SES children. In: Dziubalska-Kołaczyk, Katarzyna & Weckwerth, Jarosław (eds) *Rajendra Singh: In memoriam. Papers from a special commemorative Session at the 44th Poznań Linguistic Meeting*, Poznań: Adam Mickiewicz University Press, 25–40.

Korecky-Kröll, Katharina; Dressler, Wolfgang U.; Freiberger, Eva M.; Reinisch, Eva; Mörth, Karlheinz & Libben, Gary (2014) Morphonotactic and phonotactic processing in German-speaking adults, *Language Sciences* 46, 48–58. doi:10.1016/j.langsci.2014.06.006

Korecky-Kröll, Katharina; Freiberger, Eva M.; Dressler, Wolfgang U. & Calderone, Basilio (2016) Acquiring and processing German Words of different (mor)phonotactic structure: Morpheme boundaries inside consonant clusters delay processing, but not acquisition. 10th International Conference on the Mental Lexicon. Ottawa, 19 October 2016 (Poster).

Laine, Matti; Vainio, Seppo & Hyönä, Jukka (1999) Lexical access routes to nouns in a morphologically rich language, *Journal of Memory and Language* 40, 109–135.

Levshina, Natalia (2015) *How to do Linguistics with R: Data Exploration and Statistical Analysis.* Amsterdam, Philadelphia: John Benjamins Publishing Company.

Libben, Gary (2014) The nature of compounds: A psychocentric perspective, *Cognitive Neuropsychology* 31, 1–18.

MacWhinney, Brian (2000) *The CHILDES Project. Tools for Analyzing Talk.* Mahwah, NJ: Erlbaum.

Psychology Software Tools, Inc. [E-Prime 3.0] (2016) Retrieved from <https://support.pstnet.com>.

Sommer-Lolei, Sabine; Korecky-Kröll, Katharina & Dressler, Wolfgang U. (2017) Morphological richness and the acquisition and processing of German morphonotactic patterns. Poznań Linguistic Meeting (PLM). Poznań, 19 September 2017.

Xanthos, Aris; Laaha, Sabine; Gillis, Steven; Stephany, Ursula; Aksu-Koç, Ayhan; Christofidou, Anastasia; Gagarina, Natalia; Hrzica, Gordana; Ketrez, F. Nihan; Kilani-Schoch, Marianne; Korecky-Kröll, Katharina; Kovačević, Melita; Laalo, Klaus; Palmović, Marijan; Pfeiler, Barbara; Voeikova, Maria D. & Dressler, Wolfgang U. (2011) On the role of morphological richness in the early development of noun and verb inflection, *First Language* 31, 461–479.

Zydorowicz, Paulina (2007) Polish morphonotactics in first language acquisition, *Wiener Linguistische Gazette* 74, 24–44.

Zydorowicz, Paulina (2009) Polish and English morphonotactics in first language acquisition. In: Dziubalska-Kołaczyk, Katarzyna; Witkoś, Jacek; Michalski, Grzegorz; Wiland, Bartosz (eds) *Proceedings of the 2nd Student Conference on Formal Linguistics*. Poznań: School of English. Adam Mickiewicz University.

Zydorowicz, Paulina (2010) Consonant clusters across morpheme boundaries: Polish morphonotactic inventory and its acquisition, *Poznań Studies in Contemporary Linguistics* 46, 565–588.

Zydorowicz, Paulina & Dziubalska-Kołaczyk, Katarzyna (2017) The dynamics of marked consonant clusters in Polish. In: Babatsouli, Elena (ed.) *Proceedings of the International Symposium on Monolingual and Bilingual Speech 2017*. Chania, Greece: Institute of Monolingual and Bilingual Speech, 318–324. <http://ismbs.eu/publications-2017>.

Zydorowicz, Paulina; Kamandulytė, Laura; Freiberger, Eva M.; Korecky-Kröll, Katharina & Dressler, Wolfgang U. (2015) Morphological richness facilitates first language acquisition of morphonotactic consonant clusters: Polish and Lithuanian vs. Austrian German and English. 3rd International Workshop on Phonotactics and Phonotactic Modeling (PPM 2015). Vienna, 26 November 2015.

IV. Exploring phonotactic and morphonotactic constraints in the acquisition of consonant clusters in L1 French

BARBARA KÖPKE[1]
OLIVIER NOCAUDIE[1]
HÉLÈNE GIRAUDO[2]

1. INTRODUCTION

Consonant clusters are relatively rare in the languages of the world and count as phonologically marked (see e.g. Greenberg 1965; Clements & Keyser 1983; Maddieson 1984; Vennemann 1988; Blevins 1995; Dziubalska-Kołaczyk 2009). Nevertheless, they do figure prominently in a number of languages such as German or Polish. The fact that most of these languages are inflecting-fusional ones and that many of the clusters attested in them occur at morpheme boundaries suggests that morphological factors might be involved in the emergence and first language (L1) acquisition of clusters. In particular, the possibility that clusters may function as boundary signals (cf. already Trubetzkoy 1939) is likely to play a role.

The present study focuses on the time of emergence, position and phonotactic vs. morphonotactic status of consonant clusters (henceforth CC) in the acquisition of L1 French. In order to benefit from the growing number of resources made available by the scientific community, we selected a corpus out of the CHILDES database (MacWhinney 2000), allowing for comparison with L1 acquisition data collected to test the Strong Morphonotactic Hypothesis (SMH) for German (Freiberger 2007, 2014). We then analysed longitudinal data from four children aged 1;6 to 3;0 collected in spontaneous speech interactions between a parent and the target child with a generalized linear mixed model investigating the role of the factors age, position and phonotactic (PH) vs. morphonotactic (MPH) status on the successful pronunciation of the different CCs.

[1] LNPL – Laboratoire de NeuroPsychoLinguistique, University of Toulouse (UT2), Toulouse, France.
[2] CNRS, CLLE-ERSS, University of Toulouse (UT2).

2. CONSONANT CLUSTERS IN FIRST LANGUAGE ACQUISITION

2.1. Phonotactics and consonant clusters

A number of studies have investigated the role of phonotactics in the acquisition of the L1. It is generally assumed that phonotactics provide cues allowing the child to identify word boundaries in speech, hence conferring a key role to phonotactics in word segmentation. This is confirmed by growing evidence about how the acquisition of phonotactics bootstraps the acquisition of lexicon and grammar (cf. Boll-Avetisyan 2012). Moreover, phonotactics also play a role in adult language processing: for instance, McQueen (1998) showed that adults recognize words more rapidly when the junction between two words forms a phoneme cluster that does not typically occur within words. Such findings draw attention to the role of CCs and their significance in phonotactics since their nature and distribution varies a lot across languages.

The production of CCs has been shown to be particularly difficult in L1 acquisition, in accordance with the idea that more marked structures (Trubetzkoy 1939) will be more difficult to acquire than less marked ones. However, it has also been shown that the ease of acquisition of CCs is not homogenous and depends on a number of parameters such as syllable structure, position, frequency, morphology and input factors (e.g. Demuth & McCullough 2009), which also differ across languages. In the same vein, Levelt, Schiller and Levelt (2000) have shown that the order of acquisition of syllable structures "closely matched the frequency with which those syllable structures occurred in child-directed speech" (cited by Demuth & McCullough 2009: 427).

Structural aspects of phonotactics have been comprehensively described in the Beats-and-Binding model of Dziubalska-Kołaczyk (2002), providing a scale of preference for markedness based on overall sonority as composed of sonority, place of articulation and voicing. Studies by Demuth and collaborators on L1 acquisition also take into account sonority (e.g. Demuth & McCullough 2009). In addition, it has been suggested that syllable-initial consonants are less marked than syllable-final consonants and hence easier to acquire, the former also being present in a larger number of languages. The same should hold for CCs in an initial position, which should be easier to acquire than CCs in a final position. However, for analytic languages such as English, the contrary seems to be true, which has been explained through frequency and syllable structure effects, among other things (see Demuth 2007; or Demuth & McCullough 2009, for reviews). Data for Dutch (where word-initial and word-final clusters are about equally frequent) suggest that some children produce clusters more easily in the initial position and others in the final position.

These data suggest a strong link between the acquisitional process and the structure of the target language. Demuth and McCullough (2009) have challenged these predictions with respect to French, based on the idea that analyses of child-directed speech show that around 70% of CCs are in the word-initial position, predicting a frequency advantage for word-initial clusters. This hypothesis is investigated with the analysis of the speech production of two children (Tim and Marie from the Lyon Corpus recorded by Demuth & Tremblay 2008) recorded repeatedly between ages 1;5 and 3;0. The results show higher accuracy in the production of word-initial CCs than word-final CCs as predicted, and this independently of syllable structure factors such as sonority. The study furthermore showed that word-medial CCs were produced with roughly the same accuracy as word-initial CCs in French.

2.2. Morphonotactics and consonant clusters

Apart from frequency and structurally based factors, morphological structure has also been supposed to play a role in the acquisition of CCs. For example, Kirk and Demuth (2005) examined the production of CCs in an elicitation task in English-speaking two-year-olds and found that the children were more accurate in producing word-final clusters consisting of obstruent +/s/ compared to word-initial clusters (e.g. cu<u>ps</u> vs. <u>sp</u>oon) and, most interestingly, to final clusters with the same but reversed segmental content (e.g. cu<u>ps</u> vs. wa<u>sp</u>). The authors explain these results through both input-related and morphological factors: obstruent +/s/ clusters are more frequent, but most importantly (and probably linked to the first factor), they involve an inflectional (and very productive) morpheme. This could lead to a morphological advantage for final clusters, which, in turn, may help children acquiring languages such as English to focus very early on complexity at the end of the words. Furthermore, morphological effects appear very early in language perception and production. Numerous studies suggest that infants start perceiving functional morphemes at an early age. They distinguish forms of function words (free morphemes) from content words and decode specific function words during the first year of life (e.g. Shi & Werker 2003; Shi, Werker & Cutler 2006; Shi, Werker & Morgan 1999).

A recent study conducted by Marquis and Shi (2012) provided the first empirical evidence that French-learning 11-month-olds can use the encoded bound morphemes for interpreting the internal units of newly encountered words. They demonstrated that infants analyse the word-internal morphology during their first year of life before learning word meaning, and that the decoding of a bound functional morpheme depends on the morpheme frequency. This finding suggests that rudimentary representations of morphological alternations emerge very early in the long-term memory of infants. Finally, in an application of the Beats-and-Binding model to L1 acquisition, Zydorowicz (2007, 2009) has shown that Polish-speaking children reduce morphonotactic clusters less frequently than phonotactic ones, similarly to what has been shown for Lithuanian and English (Kamandulytė 2006; Kirk & Demuth 2005).

Despite such promising results, investigations of how morphotactics facilitate the acquisition of phonotactics in children are still rare. However, Dressler and Dziubalska-Kołaczyk (2006) and Dressler, Dziubalska-Kołaczyk and Pestal (2010) have elaborated a model of morphonotactics and its correspondence to phonotactics that has been tested in preliminary studies on L1 acquisition of German (Freiberger 2014). The Strong Morphonotactic Hypothesis (SMH) issued within this framework assumes that typically developing children should acquire morphonotactic clusters earlier than comparable purely phonotactic ones, because morphonotactic clusters are likely to be expressed more consistently in the input to which the children are exposed. Moreover, their segmental constituents will also occur independently of each other in phonologically less marked configurations. The investigation of morphonotactic clusters acquired during different acquisitional phases of productive morphology (cf. Bittner, Dressler & Kilani-Schoch 2003) should allow us to establish which of the two factors plays a more important role. The framework also assumes that morphonotactic clusters with many phonotactic counterparts lack a morphological signalling function. Moreover, they may often be affected by the same repair mechanisms as parallel phonotactic clusters and expressed less faithfully in the adult speech input than morphonotactic clusters with few or no phonotactic counterparts. Therefore, they also ought to be acquired less easily and during later phases. Nevertheless, adult-like production of morphonotactic clusters may precede (in terms of the first emergence or frequency of occurrence) the production of homophonous purely phonotactic clusters.

Furthermore, phonologically more marked clusters should be acquired later than less marked ones (independently of whether they are phonotactic or morphonotactic). Still, it needs to be investigated how the acquisition of morphonotactic clusters is affected by the absence or presence and also the frequency of parallel phonotactic ones. The framework also stresses that the measurement of markedness should differentiate between different positions in the word and give much consideration to ease of perception (such as the Net Auditory Distance among segments, as proposed by Dziubalska-Kołaczyk 2009).

These assumptions have been investigated by Freiberger (2014) through the analysis of a longitudinal corpus of spontaneous speech data from 3 typically developing monolingual children acquiring German as an L1 in Austria that was analysed with respect to the interaction of phonotactic and morphotactic factors. For each child, the researcher selected 30 minutes of recordings per month between age 1;6 and 3;0[3]. Three developmental phases were distinguished during this period. The data were transcribed according to CHILDES norms, all spontaneously produced clusters were extracted, and correctly vs. incorrectly pronounced clusters were analysed with respect to the number of consonants, position, morphonotactic vs. phonotactic status and number of morphological boundaries. The results showed the expected progression in accuracy with age and that the children had more difficulties with initial than with medial and final clusters (similarly to what has been shown for English). While morphonotactic clusters did not involve additional difficulties due to their complexity, there was no interaction between morphological and phonological factors as expected.

Given the specificities in the acquisition of morphonotactic CCs to be expected in different languages varying with respect to inflectional patterns and phonological typology, the present study seeks to complement existing data on the acquisition of CCs in Polish, German, English and Lithuanian with data from French that, as a Romance language, can be expected to show a different acquisitional path. While some data exist on phonotactic factors, previous studies on CC acquisition in French have not taken morphological factors into account.

3. METHODOLOGY

The aim of the present study was to explore the acquisition of CCs by L1 French children, their time of emergence and speed of acquisition, as well as to scrutinize aspects of the SMH (Dressler & Dziubalska-Kołaczyk 2006) in L1 French acquisition. In order to provide data that

[3] One of the children was recorded from age 1;3, allowing the author to take into account a fourth developmental stage, T0, for this child.

can be compared to other related studies within this framework, the methodology chosen is based on a replication of Freiberger's (2014) analysis of a corpus with data from 3 children aged 1;6 to 3;0.

3.1. Corpus selection

An increasing number of resources on L1 acquisition have been made available to the scientific community in recent years. For the present study, we referred to the CHILDES database (MacWhinney 2000) and selected a corpus with a comparable recording process to the methodology used by Freiberger (2014) in order to test the SMH in L1 German acquisition. The criteria we used were the recording of spontaneous speech interactions between a parent and the target child, an age of onset of 1;6 and regular recordings up to 3;0. The corpus recorded by Demuth and Tremblay (2008) (hereafter 'Lyon Corpus') meets these requirements: four children were, on average, recorded bimonthly (Anaïs, Marie, Nathan and Theotime) from an age onset of 1;0 to the age of 3;0 (4;0 for Marie) and the children's utterances have been orthographically and phonetically transcribed in CHAT format (MacWhinney 2000). The data of one of the children (Marie) had already been analysed with respect to the acquisition of CCs (together with data from Tim in Demuth & McCullough 2009). A further advantage of the Lyon Corpus is that data for child-directed speech are available from the mothers of the children.

3.2. Methodology and characteristics of the corpus

The data analysed here are summarized in Table 1. We have analysed 18 recordings per child for Anaïs, Marie and Theotime and 20 recordings for Nathan. The table shows that the number of word tokens is highly variable from one child to another – as can be expected in this age group – ranging from 6,396 tokens (Nathan) to 22,729 tokens (Anaïs). First of all, we analysed the orthographic transcription of the corpus. To start with, we performed a frequency count of each lexical item transcribed from these recordings and sorted all words containing CCs with the help of the FREQ command in CLAN (freq*.cha +t*CHI) followed by manual extraction of the targets. The following tokens were excluded from this analysis: some complex lexical units (*parce que* 'because')[4], proper

[4] In what follows, we provide English translations for the French lexical units, but not for proper names and interjections or onomatopoeia.

names (*Amtaro*) and onomatopoeia (*vroum*). The analysis shows that infant speech in French involves an interesting, albeit also variable proportion of words containing CCs ranging from 4.4% for Anaïs to 10.6% for Theotime).

Table 1. Number of recordings and tokens per child, percentages of CC tokens in the corpus

Child	Recordings (age)	Total number of word tokens	CC (% of total)
Anaïs	18 (1;0–3;0)	22,729	1023 (4.50%)
Marie	18 (1;0–4;0)	19,496	1642 (8.42%)
Nathan	20 (1;0–3;0)	6,396	464 (7.25%)
Theotime	18 (1;0–3;0)	20,150	2140 (10.62%)

Further analysis of the words produced by two of the children (Marie and Nathan) demonstrates the variety of CCs found in the speech of the children. Table 2 presents a summary of the cluster combinations according to consonant type of the first and the second consonant. Unsurprisingly, the table clearly shows that combinations of plosives and liquids are most frequent in infant speech (see also Demuth & McCullough 2009). The data also provide evidence for the presence of some more complex clusters involving three or four consonants (see Table 3).

Table 2. Variety of CCs in Marie and Nathan‘s recordings

C2 / C1	Fricative	Plosive	Liquid
Fricative	/sf/	/ʃk/ /sk/ /sp/ /st/	/fl/ fr/ /zl/ /vr/
Plosive	/ks/ /ps/ /tʃ/	/gb/ /kt/ /mt/ /pt/	/bl/ /br/ /dr/ /gl/ /gr/ / kl/ /kr/ /pl/ /pr/ /tr/
Liquid	/ls/ /rs/ /rʃ/ /rz/ / rʒ/ /rv/	/ld/ /lk/ /lm/ /ln/ /lt/ /rb/ /rd/ / rg/ /rk/ /rm/ /rn/ /rp/ /rt/	/rl/

Table 3. CCs with 3 or more consonant sounds in Marie's and Nathan's recordings

3+ CCs
/kspl/ /kspr/ /lkr/ /rbr/ /rkl/ /rsk/ /str/

We also analysed the number of CCs for different developmental stages, similarly to the analyses by Freiberger (2014). The data summarized in Table 4 show a clear progression of the number of CCs with age for each child. However, bear in mind that these data were obtained with the orthographical tier and remain hypothetical with respect to the actual production of the CCs. As such, they mainly demonstrate the diversification and complexification of the lexicon in each child.

Table 4. Number of CCs in the word tokens per child for each age group

Child	1;6–1;8	1;9–1;11	2;0–2;2	2;3–2;5	2;6–2;8	2;9–2;11	3;0–3;2
Anaïs	12	11	78	164	271	221	268
Marie	12	82	200	161	290	525	376
Nathan	6	31	20	126	69	130	82
Théo	51	213	163	399	239	648	428

Qualitative analysis of the words (see Tables I and II in appendix) shows that the first words containing CCs produced by French L1 children are from various categories with an important proportion of nouns (e.g. *nounours* 'teddy', *veste* 'jacket', échարpe 'scarf', *fleur* 'flower', *fraise* 'strawberry') and interjections/onomatopoeia (e.g. *bravo, oups, vroum, gling, clac, crac*) followed by adverbs or adverbial locutions (e.g. *s'il-te-plaît* 'please', *après* 'after', *autre* 'other', *plein* 'lots', *trop* 'too much') and verbs (e.g. *regarde* 'look', *prend* 'take', *parti* 'gone', *marche* 'walk', *ferme* 'close'), mostly in infinitive or participle constructions.

We then sorted words containing CCs that were classified as either phonotactic or morphonotactic in the productions of the four children (see Table 5). This was achieved with the FREQ command provided by CLAN. In addition, manual extraction of our targets allowed us to establish the CC's frequency in French and their phonemic variety in infant speech. Then, the CCs presented in Tables 2 and 3 were set up as targets we systematically searched for within a subset of the Lyon Corpus. This subset is composed of around 20 hours of recording for each child and balanced across different time frames. Within this subcorpus, we compared for each target token the expected phonological form and the child's actual pronunciation. Through KWAL commands followed by manual extraction, we sorted 5,276 occurrences which were categorized according to the following criteria: child, age, gender, CC group (Table 2 headers), CC (Table 2 contents), CC position (initial, medial, final), PH vs. MPH (phonotactic vs. morphonotactic cluster), grammatical class, lexical form, number of syllables, phonetic realization, CC realization (0 = error; 1 = success), and the type of CC error (reduction, substitution, omission, repetition, epenthesis, shifted cluster or mixed sounds).

Table 5. Total number of phonotactic (PH) and morphonotactic (MPH) clusters in each position for the four children

	initial	medial	final	Total
MPH		289	721	1,010
PH	1,932	1,297	1,030	4,259
Total	1,932	1,586	1,751	5,269

Table 5 shows that there are more than four times as many phonotactic clusters (N = 4,259) than morphonotactic clusters (N = 1,010) in the recordings. While PH clusters appear in all positions and even slightly more in the word-initial position, MPH clusters mostly appear in the final position and to a lesser extent in the middle of words, but not at all in the word-initial position. The latter finding is not surprising since word-initial MPH clusters are non-existent in French and consequently absent from child-directed speech (Demuth & McCullough 2009).

Table 6. Distribution of the different types of MPH clusters in word-medial and word-final position

Cluster MPH	Example	Position		Total MPH
		medial	final	
Dr	*prendre* 'take'		7	7
Rd	*regarde*[5] 'look'	58	541	599
Rk	*pourquoi* 'why'	162		162
Rm	*dormi* 'slept'	14	1	15
Rt	*parti* 'gone'	52	8	60
Sf	*transforme* 'transform'	3		3
Tr	*mettre* 'put'		164	164
Total		289	721	1,010

Table 6 shows the number of tokens and distribution of the different MPH clusters in the corpus. It is obvious from the data that some of the clusters are very rare and appear in only one specific word. For example,

[5] The data concerning these items have, however, to be treated with caution. First, the morphotactic status of the cluster is questionable since the different forms of the verb *regarder* 'to look' are principally opposed to the noun *regard* 'gaze' (rare in child language!), and the noun is derived from the verb, and not the other way around (Dressler, personal communication). Additionally, as we will see later, this cluster is very frequently reduced through omission of the liquid by the children, but also in child-directed speech (Demuth & McCullough 2009).

'sf' is limited to the word *transforme* 'transform' and only appears in this configuration in a word-medial position. Other clusters show high overall frequency, but again, they appear in only one very frequent token (*pourquoi* 'why', *regarde* 'look').

We then proceeded to the analysis of the phonological tier allowing us to establish the proportion of CCs correctly produced. Table 7 recapitulates the percentage of correctly produced clusters for each child in the different developmental stages. The high variability across the children is striking. While two of the children (Marie and Theotime) reach more than 80% correct performances by age 3, the proportion is only 40% for Nathan (and not yet stable), and it does not exceed 10% for Anaïs, for whom no real progression is evident over the recording periods. Furthermore, it cannot be excluded that the actual production of CCs is related to the use of words containing CCs, the two children obtaining the highest mastery of CCs also being those who produce the most words containing them (see Table 4). However, it also has to be noted that Anaïs, who shows clear difficulties with CCs, seems to be rather talkative, as indicated by the number of tokens produced (see Table 1).

Table 7. Percentage of correctly produced consonant clusters per child and per age group

Child	1;6–1;8	1;9–1;11	2;0–2;2	2;3–2;5	2;6–2;8	2;9–2;11	3;0–3;2
Anaïs	0	9.09	2.56	0.61	9.96	4.98	10.07
Marie	0	10.98	9.00	34.78	57.24	81.14	80.05
Nathan	0	3.23	10.00	3.17	14.49	14.62	40.24
Theotime	7.84	41.31	61.35	70.68	81.97	87.96	84.11

We then applied a generalized linear mixed model investigating the role of the following factors: age, position and PH vs. MPH status on the successful pronunciation of the different CCs. The results of this analysis are presented in the next section.

3.3. Statistical exploration of the factors favouring successful pronunciation of CCs

For the statistical exploration, a generalized linear mixed model was chosen because our data consider a binary nominal variable (is a CC produced correctly or not) in relationship with a list of factors, some of these being random (e.g. the child's proficiency or the difficulty in pronouncing a CC) and others considered as independent variables (e.g. PH/MPH status).

With such a model, the slope of the logit is modelled over time (that is, the fixed effect on the probability that a CC is correctly produced), depending on the position of the CC, its PH or MPH status, the number of syllables in the word, and so on. We have defined two types of random effects:

- the children (who are more or less performant [1])
- the CC types (which are more or less difficult to produce and more or less frequent [2])

Model 0 inspected the evolution of performance depending on the age of the children. The 4 children and all 10 CC classes (e.g. *liquid+plosive* or *plosive+obstruent*) were taken as random effects in the model. The results show that with growing age, the probability of a 'correct' answer increases significantly (β = 0.63, p = 0.001), as can be expected with typically developing children. Figure 1 represents the probability slope that should be expected for any child, following Model 0's data.

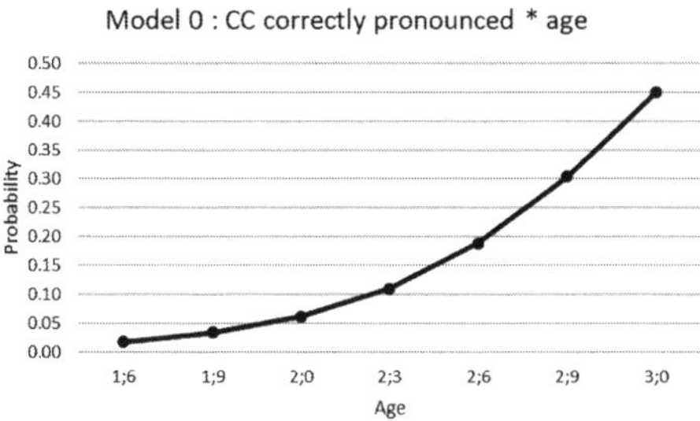

Figure 1. Percentage of consonant clusters correctly pronounced per age group (Model 0)

For Model 1, we added the morphonotactic status of the CC (PH vs. MPH) to the factor age and took into account the possible interactions between these factors. As for Model 0, an increase in age results in an increase of the probability that a CC is correctly produced (β = 0.71, p = 0.001). The model also suggests that the MPH status over all age groups had a positive effect on the pronunciation of CCs (β = 0.72, p = 0.02). However, the negative interaction between the factor age and MPH status tempers this result (β = -0.37, p = 0.001). To refine these first results, and as MPH CCs are not spread evenly across positions in the word, the following statistical models take into account the position of the CC in the word.

Model 2 considered the CCs located in the word-initial position as well as the age groups. As CCs in this position cannot have MPH status, the latter factor was excluded from the model. Model 2 reports a positive effect of increasing age ($\beta = 0.59$, $p = 0.001$) and the initial position of the CC ($\beta = 0.75$, $p < 0.01$) on the success of pronunciation of a CC. The interaction between these two factors also has a positive, albeit slight, effect ($\beta = 0.15$, $p = 0.001$).

Model 3 investigated CCs located in the word-medial position, age groups, and the CC's MPH status. Again, rising age results in an increase in the probability that a CC will be pronounced correctly ($\beta = 0.63$, $p = 0.001$). Nonetheless, when considered alone, the MPH status of the CC ($\beta = -1.39$, $p = 0.001$) and the medial position of CCs ($\beta = -0.73$, $p < 0.01$) seems to decrease the chance that a CC will be produced correctly. If we now consider the interactions in Model 3, there is a positive interaction between MPH status*medial position ($\beta = 1.76$, $p = 0.001$) with respect to correct pronunciation of the CC, while a less pronounced positive effect is observed for the age*CC's medial position interaction ($\beta = 0.20$, $p < 0.01$).

Finally, Model 4 focused on the CCs in the word-final position, while also taking into account age and MPH status. The age factor remained, once again, the major effect ($\beta = 0.80$, $p = 0.001$) in the model. When isolated, factors such as the final position and MPH status had no significant effect in this model. However, the interactions age*final position ($\beta = -0.35$, $p = 0.001$) and MPH status*final position ($\beta = -0.54$, $p = <0.05$) showed a moderate negative effect on the probability that a CC will be produced correctly.

To summarize our results, the statistical analysis showed that the factor age was the most important influence on the children's output, as can be expected from typically developing children. Concerning the CC's position in the word, French children tend overall to a left-side preference in the development of the pronunciation of CCs, with word-initial CCs tending to be produced correctly at an earlier age. As for the CC's MPH status, our models observed that only MPH clusters in a medial position (and probably specifically for the latest age group considered here) had positive effects on the success of pronunciation of clusters. That being said, it must be kept in mind that these results may be influenced by several factors inherent to our corpus:

- MPH clusters are relatively scarce in French words, and even more so in children's spontaneous speech corpora;
- MPH clusters occur only in a limited number of words, but these are likely to be very frequent French words, such as *pourquoi*

'why' with a cluster in the medial position, or *regarde*[6] 'look', in imperative mode, with a cluster in the final position. If *regarde* is used as a deictic from very early on (543 tokens, from age 1;6 in the corpus) by both children and caregivers, *pourquoi* (162 tokens, from age 2;0 in the corpus) emerges later in the child lexicon, i.e. at a more advanced developmental stage.

Nevertheless, the results also showed that there is a lot of variation among the children, which is why the next section seeks to explore further the individual developmental trajectories.

3.4. Exploration of the individual developmental trajectories

The developmental trajectories for each of the four children were explored with reference to the type of the given responses, first for all CCs and then specifically for MPH clusters. The results for overall CC production (see Figure 2) illustrate the inter-individual differences: while two of the children (Anaïs and Nathan) produce hardly any correct clusters during the entire period of investigation (1;6–3;0), the other two (Marie and Theotime) show a steady increase in correct production from age 2;0 (Marie) and age 1;6 (Theotime) respectively. Additionally, error patterns are also interesting and demonstrate a specific trajectory for each child. While substitutions are rare in the production of all four, the children differ considerably with respect to the amount and distribution of the other error types. Theotime is very performant from the beginning, and omissions of CCs are rare in his speech even at the first recording, and remain close to zero thereafter. By preference he uses reductions of CCs, but even these are exceeded by correct productions from as early as around age 1;8. Both Nathan and Marie start with 100% omissions at age 1;6, but these are caught up by reductions at around age 1;8 for Marie and 2;4 for Nathan. Anaïs, who shows the most severe difficulties with CCs, has a quite different distribution of these two error types: from the beginning, she produces more reductions than omissions, and despite a lot of variation in the different recordings, this does not change substantially over the period investigated.

We then looked specifically at the distribution of these error types and the correct productions of CCs in MPH clusters only (see Figure 3). Anaïs' CC productions remain close to zero during the whole investiga-

[6] But see our reservations about the MPH status of the final cluster in *regarde* in note 3 (section 2.2).

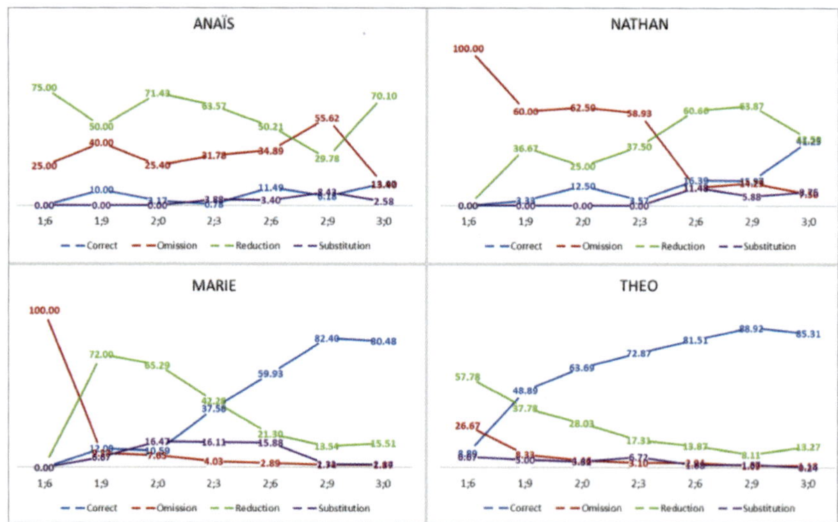

Figure 2. Percentage of occurrence of each type of CC event coded in the corpus for each child/age group. Correctly produced CC (blue), CC omission (red), CC reduction (green), CC substitution (purple).

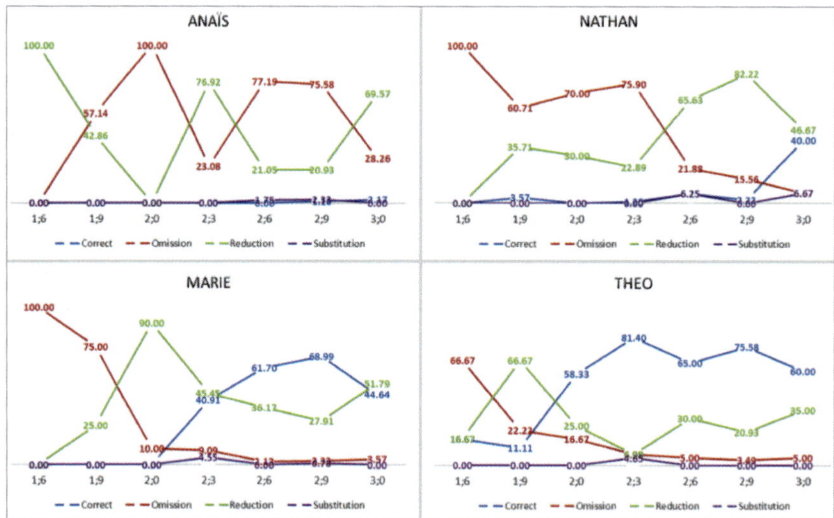

Figure 3. Percentage of occurrence of each type of event coded in the corpus for MPH clusters only * child * age group. Correctly produced CC (blue), CC omission (red), CC reduction (green), CC substitution (purple)

tion period, while errors seem to be distributed randomly between reductions and omissions. In Nathan's speech, correctly pronounced MPH CCs appear only at the end of the period, from age 2;9 onwards, and reductions start to exceed omissions from around age 2;5 onwards. Marie shows a similar pattern, but much earlier: correct productions appear at age 2;0 and the number of reductions exceed the omissions from around age 1;10. For Theotime the trajectory here is more similar to the pattern shown by Nathan and Marie, but even earlier than Marie and with higher success rates. Despite the high variability across children, these data suggest that there is an overall developmental pattern with the number of omissions decreasing while the number of reductions increases across the age groups.

4. DISCUSSION

The results of our data analysis are in line with the other studies on the acquisition of consonant clusters in French, showing that all these clusters are subject to different types of modifications (namely reduction to the least sonorous segment, gliding, insertion of schwa, etc.) before they are produced in a target-like manner. This has been documented, for example, in the study conducted by Andreassen (2013) on 13 monolingual children aged 2;2–3;2 years. The data are also consistent with the studies on CC acquisition in general (for a review, see McLeod, van Doorn & Reed 2001) showing that CCs emerge very progressively around age 2 (e.g. French 1989; Lléo & Prinz 1996, for Spanish and German). Overall, the studies on CC acquisition suggest that production of CCs starts around age 2, but, independently of the target language, their production is rarely correct at that age. Additionally, the age of mastery seems to be highly variable across children, as also documented by the data from the four children we considered in this study showing considerable variation in the correct CC productions of, for instance, Anaïs (10.07% correct at age 3;0–3;2) and Theotime (84.11% correct at the same age). With regard to American English, Shriberg and Kwiatkowski (1980) observed 90% correct at age 4, while Smit el al. (1990), on the contrary, report that only few productions were correct at age 4. In their sample the majority of CCs seemed to be mastered at age 6 or 7, though some difficulties persisted even up to age 8 or 9.

Among the factors generally found to influence the age of mastery of pronunciation are the position and structure of the cluster. Yet the observations made with respect to these factors are still inconsistent. For example, McLeod and colleagues, in an extensive literature review on CC acquisition, state that "In languages other than English, word-final CC have been reported to be acquired before word-initial clusters" (McLeod et al. 2001: 101). However, as regards French, word-initial clusters tend to be produced earlier than word-final clusters (see Demuth & McCullough 2009; Kirk & Demuth 2005). While it is also acknowledged that the position no longer matters in older children, such inconsistencies between studies need to be elucidated.

Additionally, McLeod et al. (2001) suggest that clusters involving plosive+liquid are easier to acquire than clusters involving fricative+liquid. This is in line with what has been observed by Demuth and colleagues (Demuth & McCullough 2009; Demuth & Tremblay 2008) for the acquisition of CCs in French. However, there are also a number of other, less investigated factors that are likely to play a role in language-specific acquisition trajectories: the syllable structure, foot structure, frequency (e.g. Kehoe et al. 2008), saliency (Baroni 2014) and the primary and secondary status of the cluster (Andreassen 2013). For instance, there is a strong tendency for French towards monosyllabism resulting in a reduced number of morphemes per words and hence in fewer morphological boundaries and reduced morphonotactics.

Concerning our main research questions, the findings of the present study suggest that there are differences in the processing of MPH and PH clusters in the acquisition of L1 French. These are, however, modulated by the fact the MPH clusters mainly appear in the word-final position in French (and to a lesser extent in a medial position), a position that seems, for other reasons, to be less favourable in early acquisition. The observations we made are consistent with the predictions of the SMH in respect of the phonological and morphological characteristics of French (Dressler & Dziubalska-Kołaczyk 2006). From a phonological point of view, French is a largely vocalic language and, as such, has only a limited number of consonant clusters. On the morphological side, French is one of the weakest inflecting languages among the fusional languages (at least as far as oral French is concerned). Consequently, and as predicted by morphonotactics, the number of MPH clusters is rather low, at least in the vocabulary of the age groups investigated in the present study, and results have to be treated with caution. In order to counterbalance frequency effects, it might be interesting to compare data from younger children acquiring languages with many MPH clusters with older children acquiring languages with few MPH clusters.

Another issue that needs to be discussed is the actual presence of the investigated clusters in child-directed speech to which these children are exposed. Recent studies on speech directed to French infants suggest that French parents tend to reduce omission of schwa when addressing their young children (e.g. Andreassen 2011; Liégeois, Saddour & Chabanal 2015). Reduced omission of liquids in consonant clusters has also been reported for child-directed speech in connection with one of the children investigated in the present study in respect of word-initial clusters, where parents tend to produce more complete clusters when addressing their young children compared to their usage in adult-directed speech (Demuth & McCullough 2009). However, things seem to be more variable with regard to word-final clusters: while the results of the same study showed very low omission rates for /R/-plosive clusters (e.g. *barbe* 'beard' in our corpus – with the exception of *regarde* 'look', one of the most frequent productions in our corpus where omission rates are fairly high), omission rates were high for final plosive-/R/ clusters (75% for Marie's mother, e.g. *autre* 'other'). This suggests that the advantage observed for the acquisition of word-initial CCs is not only due to overall frequency but also to the fact that word-final clusters are often phonetically reduced in the input (see Demuth & McCullough 2009, for more details).

5. CONCLUSION AND PERSPECTIVES

Based on a longitudinal corpus analysis of natural data from four children, the present study provides preliminary data on the scope of the SMH (Dressler & Dziubalska-Kołaczyk 2006) as regards French. In accordance with the predictions of the SMH, our data show that the morphonological status of a CC does not *per se* facilitate its acquisition, which is largely modulated through other factors such as frequency and position in the word, at least in the initial developmental stages investigated in the present study. However, of course, the present investigation has only permitted a preliminary exploration of the issue of the interaction of phonological and morphological aspects in the development of CCs in French. An extension of the study to later developmental stages in older children, allowing us to weight the influence of frequency, is clearly one of the primary perspectives arising from the present investigation. It would also be interesting to look more closely into the processing cost with regard to the processing of inflected forms without clusters and to inspect error patterns related to PH/MPH status of CCs.

ACKNOWLEDGEMENTS

The present study was made possible through financial support from an ANR grant n° ANR-13-ISH2-0002-02 to Basilio Calderone for the Cooperation Project 'Human Behaviour and Machine Simulation in the Processing of (Mor)Phonotactics'. We would also like to thank Wolfgang U. Dressler for helpful comments on an earlier version of the paper and Sabine Sommer-Lolei and Nicola Wood for careful editing. All remaining errors are ours.

REFERENCES

Andreassen, Helene N. (2011) La recherche de régularités distributionnelles pour la catégorisation du schwa en français (The search for distributional regularities for the categorisation of schwa in French), *Langue française* 169, 55–78.

Andreassen, Helene N. (2013) The behaviour of secondary consonant clusters in Swiss French child language, *Nordlyd* 40(1), 1–19.

Baroni, Antonio (2014) On the importance of being noticed: the role of acoustic salience in phonotactics (and casual speech), *Language Sciences* 46, 18–36.

Bittner, Dagmar; Dressler, Wolfgang U. & Kilani-Schoch, Marianne (2003) *Development of verb inflection in first language acquisition: a cross-linguistic perspective.* [Studies on Language Acquisition 21]. Berlin: De Gruyter Mouton.

Blevins, Juliette (1995) The syllable in phonological theory. In: Goldsmith, John A. (ed.) *The Handbook of Phonological Theory*. Oxford: Blackwell, 206–244.

Boll-Avetisyan, Natalie A. T. (2012) *Phonotactics and Its Acquisition, Representation, and Use. An experimental phonological study*. PhD dissertation, Utrecht University.

Clements, George N. & Keyser, Samuel J. (1983) *CV Phonology: A generative Theory of the Syllable*. Cambridge, MA: MIT Press.

Demuth, Katherine (2007) The role of frequency in language acquisition. In: Gülzow, Insa & Gagarina, Natalia (eds) *Frequency Effects in Language Acquisition: Defining the Limits of Frequency as an Explanatory Concept.* [Studies on Language Acquisition 32]. Berlin: De Gruyter Mouton, 383–388.

Demuth, Katherine & McCullough, Elizabeth (2009) The longitudinal development of clusters in French, *Journal of Child Language* 36, 425–448.

Demuth, Katherine & Tremblay, Anne (2008) Prosodically-conditioned variability in children's production of French determiners, *Journal of Child Language* 35, 99–127.

Dressler, Wolfgang U. & Dziubalska-Kołaczyk, Katarzyna (2006) Proposing Morphonotactics, *Italian Journal of Linguistics* 18(2), 249–266.

Dressler, Wolfgang U.; Dziubalska-Kołaczyk, Katarzyna & Pestal, Lina (2010) Change and variation in morphonotactics, *Folia Linguistica Historica* 31, 51–67.

Dziubalska-Kołaczyk, Katarzyna (2002) *Beats-and-Binding Phonology*. Frankfurt: Peter Lang.

Dziubalska-Kołaczyk, Katarzyna (2009) NP extension: B&B phonotactics, *PSiCL* 45, 55–73.

Freiberger, Eva M. (2007) Morphonotaktik im Erstspracherwerb des Deutschen (Morphonotactics in first language acquisition of German), *Wiener Linguistische Gazette* 74, 1–23.

Freiberger, Eva M. (2014) Der Erwerb von Konsonantenclustern im Deutschen: Eine Untersuchung longitudinaler Spontansprachkorpora (The acquisition of consonant clusters in German: an investigation of longitudinal spontaneous speech corpora), *Slowakische Zeitschrift für Germanistik* 6(2), 5–23.

French, Ann (1989) The systematic acquisition of word forms by a child during the first-fifty-word stage, *Journal of Child Language* 16, 69–90.

Greenberg, Joseph (1965) Some generalizations concerning initial and final consonant sequences, *Linguistics* 18, 5–32.

Kamandulytė, Laura (2006) The acquisition of morphonotactics in Lithuanian, *Wiener Linguistische Gazette* 73, 88–96.

Kehoe, Margaret; Hilaire-Debove, Geraldine; Demuth, Katherine & Lléo, Conxita (2008) The structure of branching onsets and rising diphthongs: Evidence from the acquisition of French and Spanish, *Language Acquisition* 15(1), 5–57.

Kirk, Cecilia & Demuth, Katherine (2005) Asymmetries in the acquisition of word-initial and word-final consonant clusters, *Journal of Child Language* 32, 709–734.

Levelt, Clara C.; Schiller, Niels O. & Levelt, Willem J. (2000) The acquisition of syllable types, *Language Acquisition* 8, 237–264.

Liégeois, Loïc; Saddour, Inès & Chabanal, Damien (2015) L'acquisition du schwa en français L1: Analyse de corpus denses d'interactions parents-enfant (The acquisition of schwa in French L1: Analysis of dense corpora of parent-child interactions), *LINX Corpus et Apprentissages du Français: Approches et Pratiques* 68–69, 49–68.

Lléo, Conxita & Prinz, Michael (1996) Consonant clusters in child phonology and the directionality of syllable structure assignment, *Journal of Child Language* 23, 31–56.

Maddieson, Ian (1984) *Patterns of sounds*. Cambridge: Cambridge University Press.

Marquis, Alexandra & Shi, Rushen (2012) Initial morphological learning in preverbal infants, *Cognition* 122, 61–66.

McLeod, Sharynne; van Doorn, Jan & Reed, Vicki A. (2001) Normal acquisition of consonant clusters, *Journal of Speech and Language Pathology* 10(2), 99–110.

McQueen, James M. (1998) Segmentation of continuous speech using phonotactics, *Journal of Memory and Language* 39, 21–46.

MacWhinney, Brian (2000) *The CHILDES Project: Tools for Analyzing Talk.* 3rd Edition. Mahwah, NJ: Lawrence Erlbaum Associates.

Shi, Rushen & Werker, Janet F. (2003) Basis of preference for lexical words in six-month-old infants, *Developmental Science* 6, 484–488.

Shi, Rushen; Werker, Janet F. & Cutler, Anne (2006) Recognition and representation of function words in English-learning infants, *Infancy* 10(2), 187–198.

Shi, Rushen; Werker, Janet F. & Morgan, James L. (1999) Newborn infants' sensitivity to perceptual cues to lexical and grammatical words, *Cognition* 72(2), B11–B21.

Shriberg, Lawrence D. & Kwiatkowski, Joan (1980) *Natural Process Analysis: A procedure for phonological analysis of continuous speech samples*. New York, NY: Macmillan.

Smit, Ann B.; Hand, Linda; Freilinger, Joseph J.; Bernthal, John E. & Bird, Ann (1990) The Iowa articulation norms project and its Nebraska replication, *Journal of Speech and Hearing Disorders* 55, 779–798.

Trubetzkoy, Nikolaï S. (1939) *Grundzüge der Phonologie* (Main features of phonology). Prague: Travaux du Cercle Linguistique de Prague, 7.

Vennemann, Theo (1988) *Preference Laws for Syllable Structure and the Explanation of Sound Change*. Berlin: De Gruyter Mouton.

Zydorowicz, Paulina (2007) Polish morphonotactics in first language acquisition, *Wiener Linguistische Gazette* 74, 24–44. <http://www.univie.ac.at/linguistics/publications/wlg/index.htm>.

Zydorowicz, Paulina (2009) Polish and English morphonotactics in first language acquisition. In: Dziubalska-Kolaczyk, Katarzyna; Witkos, Jacek; Michalski, Grzegorz; Wiland, Bartosz (eds) *Proceedings of the 2nd Student Conference on Formal Linguistics*. Poznań: School of English, Adam Mickiewicz University.

APPENDIX

Table I. Types of clusters starting with fricatives or plosives and their representations per position, their PH or MPH status, number and proportion

Cluster Group	FRI+FRI	FRI+PLO	FRI+LIQ	PLO+FRI	PLO+LIQ			PLO+PLO
Cluster	sf	sk	fl	ks	bl	gr	pr	gb
Exemple	transformé	casquette	fleur	coccinelle	blanc	gros	après	rugby
Position(s)	n_y_n	y_y_y	y_y_y	n_y_n	y_y_y	y_y_y	y_y_y	n_y_n
PH_MPH	n_y	y_n	y_n	y_n	y_n	y_n	y_n	y_n
Count (%)	3 (0.06)	102 (1.93)	46 (0.87)	24 (0.45)	196 (3.71)	364 (6.9)	271 (5.14)	1 (0.02)
Cluster		sp	fr	tʃ	br	kl	tr	kt
Exemple		aspirateur	fraise	atchoum	zèbre	clé	autre	docteur
Position(s)		y_y_n	y_y_y	n_y_y	y_y_y	y_y_y	y_y_y	n_y_y
PH_MPH		y_n	y_n	y_n	y_n	y_n	y_y	y_n
Count (%)		34 (0.64)	88 (1.67)	8 (0.15)	127 (2.41)	56 (1.06)	1135 (21.51)	17 (0.32)
Cluster		st	zl	gz	dr	kr		pt
Exemple		veste	puzzle	exemple	chaudron	crocodile		hélicoptère
Position(s)		y_y_y	n_n_y	n_y_n	y_y_y	y_y_y		n_y_n
PH_MPH		y_n	y_n	y_n	y_y	y_n		y_n
Count (%)		51 (0.97)	15 (0.28)	1 (0.02)	86 (1.63)	295 (5.59)		20 (0.8)
Cluster			vr		gl	pl		
Exemple			vroum		igloo	plein		
Position(s)			y_y_y		y_y_y	y_y_y		
PH_MPH			y_n		y_n	y_n		
Count (%)			109 (2.07)		47 (0.89)	385 (7.3)		

Table II. Types of clusters starting with liquids and their representations per position, their PH or MPH status, number and proportion

Cluster Group	LIQ+FRI		LIQ+PLO				LIQ+LIQ	3+	
Cluster	rs	rz	lk	rb	rk	rp	rl	kspl	rbr
Exemple	morceau	quatorze	quelqu'un	barbe	pourquoi	écharpe	parle	expliquent	arbre
Position(s)	n_y_y	n_y_y	n_y_y	n_y_y	n_y_y	n_y_y	n_y_y	n_y_n	n_y_y
PH_MPH	y_n	y_n	y_n	y_n	y_y	y_n	y_n	y_n	y_n
Count (%)	161 (3.05)	4 (0.08)	9 (0.17)	13 (0.25)	188 (3.56)	31 (0.59)	12 (0.23)	1 (0.02)	11 (0.21)
Cluster	rʃ	rʒ	lm	rd	rm	rt		kspr	rkl
Exemple	marche	argent	filmer	regarde	ferme	parti		exprès	couvercle
Position(s)	n_y_y	n_y_y	n_y_y	n_y_y	n_y_y	n_y_y		n_y_n	n_n_y
PH_MPH	y_n	y_n	y_n	y_y	y_n	y_y		y_n	y_n
Count (%)	150 (2.84)	39 (0.74)	2 (0.04)	642 (12.17)	80 (1.52)	247 (4.68)		2 (0.04)	2 (0.04)
Cluster		rv	lt	rg	rn			lkr	str
Exemple		servi	adulte	escargot	tourne			velcro	monstre
Position(s)		n_y_y	n_n_y	n_y_n	n_y_y			n_y_n	y_y_y
PH_MPH		y_n	y_n	y_n	y_n			y_n	y_n
Count (%)		17 (0.32)	2 (0.04)	40 (0.76)	140 (2.65)			1 (0.02)	2 (0.04)

V. The natural perceptual salience of affixes is not incompatible with a central view of morphological processing

Hélène Giraudo[1]
Karla Orihuela[1]
Basilio Calderone[1]
Barbara Köpke[2]

1. INTRODUCTION

The Strong Morphonotactic Hypothesis (Dressler & Dziubalska-Kołaczyk 2006) assumes that phonotactics helps in the decomposition of words into morphemes. Accordingly, sequences occurring over a morpheme boundary (e.g. mords, mordent, mordre /mɔʁ/ /mɔʁd/ /mɔʁdʁ/) correspond to a prototypical morphonotactic sequence that should be processed faster and more accurately than phonotactic sequences (e.g. ordre /ɔʁdʁ/).

While this issue is usually explored within studies on typical and atypical first language acquisition, a recent study carried out by Korecky-Kröll et al. (2014) tested this hypothesis with German-speaking adults. One experiment using a letter search task (i.e. find a letter like, for example, *T* at different positions – initial, medial, final – in a visual word like *Taube* 'dove', *dank-te* 'thanked' and *pack-t* '(s/he) packs') investigated whether sublexical letter sequences were found faster when the target sequence was separated from the word stem by a morphological boundary (e.g. *pack-t*) than when it was a part of a morphological root (e.g. *Lift* 'lift'). The results showed that the presence of a morpheme boundary led to shorter reaction times (RTs) and fewer errors, whatever the target cluster position in the word. The authors concluded that phonotactics helps in the decomposition of words into morphemes without, however, explicitly considering that it is a direct consequence of a morphological decomposition mechanism taking place during lexical access.

More recently, Beyersmann et al. (2014) examined the morpho-orthographic hypothesis according to which all complex forms are segmented into morphemes during lexical access. The prefixed and suffixed let-

[1] CNRS, CLLE-ERSS, University of Toulouse (UT2).
[2] LNPL – Laboratoire de NeuroPsychoLinguistique, University of Toulouse (UT2).

ter strings they manipulated comprised real stems and affixes but never formed an existing word in French (e.g. *propoint, filmure*). They used a letter search task in which adult French speakers had to decide whether the target letter was present or absent in a string of letters (e.g. 'R' in *p**r**opoint* or *filmu**r**e*). The results revealed that the letter search took longer in suffixes compared with non-suffix endings but not for prefixes compared with non-prefix beginnings. Moreover, performance was not affected by letter cluster frequency. The difference in processing suffixes relative to non-suffixes was interpreted as reflecting a chunking/affix stripping mechanism (cf. Taft & Forster's serial hypothesis 1975) that operates on functional units such as suffixes during lexical access. Furthermore, the authors interpreted the absence of effects for the prefixed non-words (i.e. no significant difference between pre-fixed and non-prefixed non-words) in terms of the different semantic and syntactic functions of prefixes relative to suffixes.

Giraudo and Grainger (2003) also found an asymmetry in the processing of prefixed vs. suffixed words in a series of masked priming experiments conducted with French complex words. More precisely, they found morphological masked priming effects, but only for prefixed words (i.e. *enjeu* 'stake' primed *envol* 'flight', while *ennui* 'boredom', a pseudo-complex in which *en-* is not a prefix and *lapin* 'rabbit', an unrelated word, did not induce any priming effect), suggesting that only prefix series are activated at the very early stages of visual word recognition. The authors interpreted this asymmetrical processing in terms of the different linguistic functions these two types of affixes imply, in particular the fact that prefixes usually carry more transparent semantic information than suffixes, whose function is much more related to syntax. Accordingly, morphological priming effects using affixed words would rely on the semantic relationships in prime-target pairs – prefix priming effects being clearly obtained. This result constitutes a challenge for decompositional models situating morphological effects at a sublexical level that should be insensitive to semantics. Moreover, the conclusions reached by Beyersmann et al. (2014) are not only contradictory to what Giraudo and Grainger (2003) found about affix processing in French but they are also incompatible with what Korecky-Kröll et al. (2014) found concerning the target cluster position, which did not interact with RTs in their experiment. Therefore, the conclusion about the kind of cognitive processes underlying affixed word analysis is not clear, while the interpretation of the effects obtained with a letter search task has to be re-examined.

As a consequence, and because Beyersmann et al. (2014) tested non-words instead of existing words, meaning that they did not control the morphonotactic characteristics of their material, it is worth carrying out a new experiment using words and controlled materials in order to tease apart the morphonotactic effects from the positional effects in word recognition. Working on non-words presents the advantage of creating the materials very easily, especially when formal aspects have to be controlled. However, working on the morphological issue, the manipulation of non-words, even if they are morphologically complex, restricts the conclusions derived from the results. First, the morphological structure of a given word actually corresponds to both the form and meaning information, and second, this word is embedded in a network formed by its morphological family and series. Therefore, the manipulation of non-words suppresses the two morphological dimensions of complex words, their syntagmatic and paradigmatic structure (see Blevins 2014 for discussion).

Finally, it is worth highlighting that, according to us, the letter search task does not permit examination of lexical access per se but rather morphological salience. Recently, Giraudo and Dal Maso (2016) discussed the issue of morphological processing through the notion of morphological salience – defined as the relative role of the word and its parts – and its implications for theories and models of morphological processing. The issue of the relative prominence of the whole word and its morphological components has indeed been overshadowed by the fact that psycholinguistic research has progressively focused on purely formal and surface features of words, drawing researchers' attention away from what morphology really is, systematic mappings between form and meaning. While we do not deny that formal features can play a role in word processing, an account of the general mechanisms of lexical access also needs to consider the perceptual and functional salience of lexical and morphological items. Consequently, if we acknowledge the sensitivity to the word's morphological structure, we claim that it corresponds to secondary and derivative units of description/analysis.

In the present research, a letter search task was carried out using French words; the main comparison is between the words that include the target letter after a morphonotactic boundary (e.g. *vivre* 'to live') and those with a purely phonotactic one (e.g. *centre* 'centre'). The hypothesis is that morphonotactic segmentation will be facilitated because of a double salience conveyed in the boundaries, as it is not only phonological but also morphological. Position effects will also be explored, as we compare the initial (position 1) vs. the final position (position 2) of letter targets. The results are presented with both a categorical analysis (comparing the different conditions) and a linear mixed-effects model.

2. METHODOLOGY

2.1. Participants

Thirty participants were recruited at the University of Toulouse, all native French speakers. The age range spanned from 18 to 30 years old (average 23); 7 were male and 23 were female. All participants were right-handed with normal or corrected to normal vision.

2.2. Items

Sixty French word forms (the same inflectional form) were used as targets; those used for the critical condition can be segmented morphotactically, while for the 3 other control conditions the syllabic segmentation was purely phonotactic (phonology and morphology did not correspond). All words included a combination of the letters 'RE', half of the time at the beginning of the word and half of the time at the end. Four conditions were created in order to counterbalance the position (initial–final), the boundary type (morphological and phonological or only phonological) of the bigram to be searched, and the part of speech status (verb or noun in singular and infinitive) of the word (see Table 1 for stimuli characteristics).

15 verbs morphonotactic (**MP verb_RE/P2**): verbs that had the letters 'RE' in a final position (after a consonant at the end of the word), and corresponded to a morphological and phonological boundary. For example, *vivre* 'to live' contains *viv-* as a morphological base (stem) and *re-* as a suffix (the infinitive mark).

15 nouns phono final (**P noun_RE/P2**): nouns that ended with 'RE', but the phonotactic boundary did not correspond to the morphological one. For example, in *centre* 'centre', *-re* is not a suffix and *cent–* is not a stem.

15 verbs phono initial (**P verb_RE/P1**): verbs that started with 'RE', but the phonotactic boundary did not correspond to the morphological one. For example, in *refuse* 'refuse' *re-* is not a prefix and *-fuse* is not a stem.

15 nouns phono initial (**P noun_RE/P1**): nouns that started with 'RE', but the phonotactic boundary did not correspond to the morphological one. For example, in *religion* 'religion' *re-* is not a prefix and *-ligion* is not a stem.

In order to perform the task, 60 filler words (30 nouns and 30 verbs) matched in length and frequency with the target words, but not having 'RE' clusters in their spelling, were used. All word frequencies were taken from the *Lexique* database (New et al. 2001).

Table 1. Stimuli controlled for frequency and length

Condition	Fx[3]	Length
Morphono (verb_P2) *vivre*	38.04	6.13
Phono (noun_P2) *centre*	32.04	6.20
Phono (verb_P1) *refuse*	30.12	6.33
Phono (verb_P1) *religion*	15.89	6.20

2.3. PROCEDURE

Participants were seated 50 cm from the computer screen and asked to perform a 'letter search task'. They were instructed to respond as rapidly and accurately as possible to whether the cluster of letters 'RE' was present or not in the word to be displayed on the screen. Participants responded 'yes' by pressing one of two response buttons with the forefinger of their right hand and 'no' by pressing the other response button with the forefinger of the left hand.

The DMDX software (Forster & Forster 2003) was used. Each trial consisted of the following sequence of stimuli: the letters to be searched (RE) presented in uppercase (for 700 ms), followed by a fixation mark (1000 ms), a French word in lowercase (50 ms), which, in turn, was replaced by a mask (##########) that remained on the screen until the participant responded (for a maximum of 1500 ms). After 10 practice trials, participants received the 120 experimental trials in one block in a randomized order (see Figure 1 for a trial example).

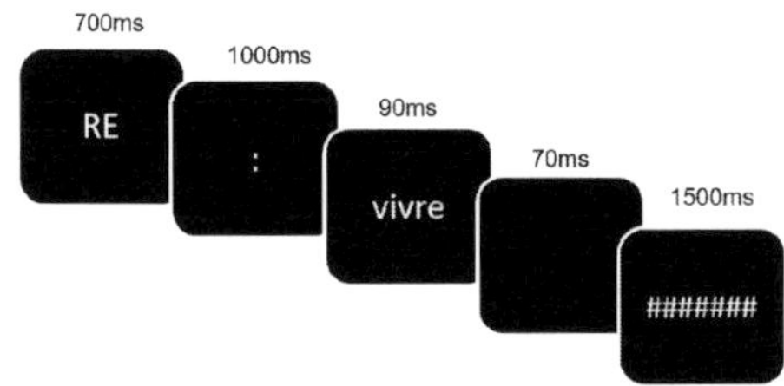

Figure 1. Trial example for the letters search task (RE)

[3] Frequency (Fx) calculated in frequency per million from the Lexique corpus database (New et al. 2001). Length corresponds to the average number of letters.

3. RESULTS 1

For the statistical analyses, filler words (with no RE clusters) are not considered. Accuracy across all participants was above 80% but no significant differences were found (see Table 2 for accuracy and reaction time means). For the reaction time (RT), trials considered 'errors' were not taken into account (6% of the data), and a trimming procedure was used: excluding responses under 300 ms (1.6% of the data) and 2.5 SDs above or below the mean response time of each participant (2.89% of the data). For the RTs (see Figure 2 for RT means), an ANOVA was conducted using participants (F1) as a random factor, treating the boundary type as a within-participant factor (repeated measures).

Table 2. Accuracy (in error rates) and reaction times (in milliseconds) means

RT	MP(verb_P2)	P(noun_P2)	P(noun_P1)	P(verb_P1)
Mean	606.20	664.38	573.55	607.18
SD	97.20	128.86	102.10	110.63
ACC	MP(verb_P2)	P(noun_P2)	P(noun_P1)	P(verb_P1)
Mean	4.67	7.56	5.11	5.33
SD	6.35	8.53	5.45	5.37

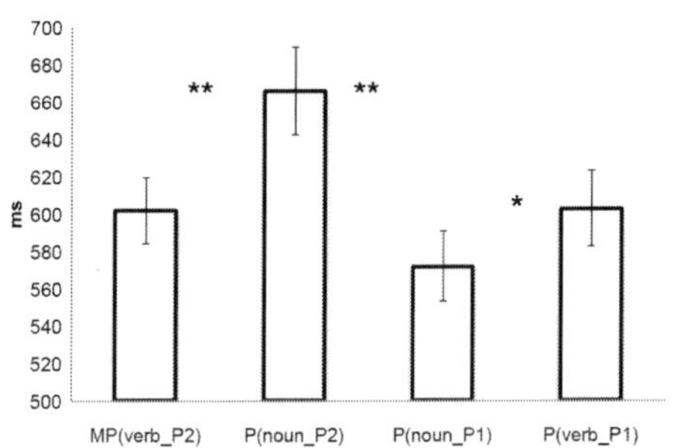

** indicates a significant difference, * indicates a trend to significance

Figure 2. Reaction time results (ms) with standard error bars (SE) of the mean for each of the different conditions

A main effect of position was found, and planned comparisons found that the only significant difference among the four conditions was that the response times for the 'MP' condition were significantly faster $F(3,59) = 8.72$ $p < .01$ than those obtained for the 'P' with RE in the first position (beginning).

Focusing on the comparison between the two conditions where the target letters were at the beginning of the word and the only difference was the boundary type, the MP condition produced a facilitation effect (over the P one). To disentangle these findings and explore whether the effects are due to the fact that these conditions differ in grammatical category (part of speech), a comparison between these variables was undertaken, but it showed no significant difference.

3.1. Position

An ANOVA revealed a significant difference between the initial and final position: $F(1,59) = 9.92$, $p < .01$, indicating that participants' responses are faster (by 76.33ms) when the target letters ('RE') are in an initial position, taking together conditions P(noun_P1) and P(verb_P1), versus when they are in a final one, MP(verb_P2) and P(noun_P2).

The average RT for the compiled values obtained for the conditions with 'RE' at the end or at the beginning of the word are shown in Table 3 and Figure 3.

Table 3. Mean average RT (and standard deviation, SD) of position (initial vs. final) in milliseconds

POSITION	RT (SD)
Initial (P1)	587.3 (133.66)
Final (P2)	633.63 (160.66)
Net Effect (P1-P2)	76.33

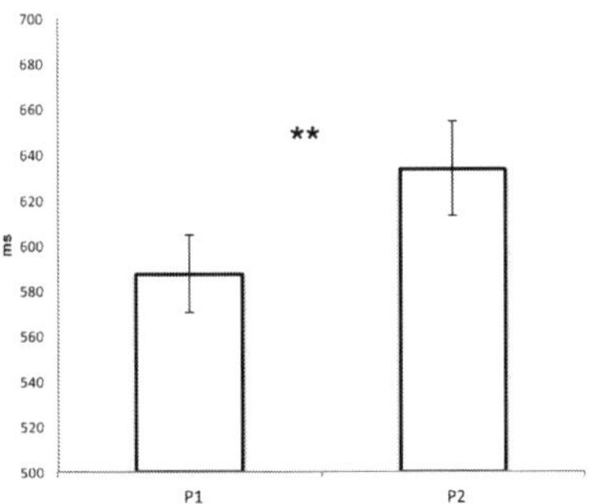

** indicates a significant difference ($p < .05$)

Figure 3. Mean average RT of position (initial vs. final) in milliseconds with SE bars

Looking only at the 'position' effect, it can be argued that 'RE' is identified faster (regardless of whether the boundary is morpho-phonological or purely phonological) when it is at the beginning of the word; this may be due to the fact that we follow a left-to-right reading direction. Nevertheless, in order to disentangle the findings, when comparing morphonotactic to merely phonotactic boundaries, there is a significant effect for the morphonotactic condition. If position is the only factor, manipulation or variable considered, then 'RE' is always found faster when at the beginning of the word but, within this position, 'RE' is found significantly faster when the boundary is morphonotactic. This is probably due to the dual information conveyed, which enhanced the morphological salience, aiding the analysis of the word into its constituents and facilitating identification of the target letters.

3.2. Part of Speech (grammatical category)

The average RT for the compiled values obtained for the conditions containing 'RE' in verbs or nouns are shown in Table 4. An ANOVA revealed no significant difference between them $F(1,59) = 1.93$, $p = .17$, indicating that even if participants' responses are slower (by 16.54 ms) when the target letters ('RE') are in a verb (condition MP_verbRE and P_RE_verb) than when they are in a noun (P_nounRe and P_RE_noun), this numerical difference is not statistically significant. The average RT for the compiled values obtained for the conditions containing 'RE' in verbs or nouns are shown in Table 4 and Figure 4.

Table 4. Mean average RT per part of speech (verb vs. noun) in milliseconds

PART OF SPEECH	RT (SD)
Verb	602.19 (136.51)
Noun	618.73 (161.22)
Net Effect (V-N)	-16.54

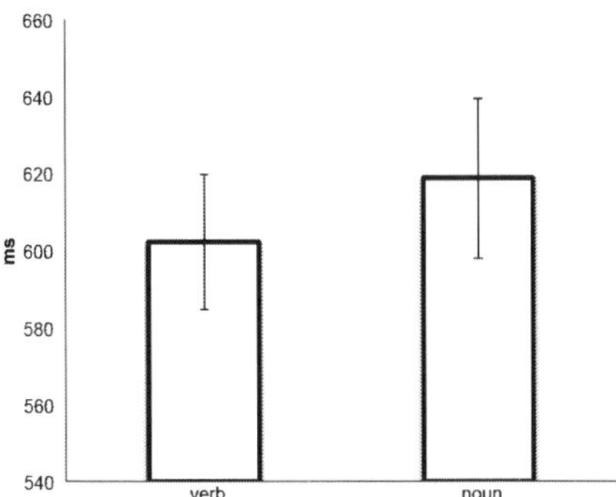

Figure 4. Mean average RT per part of speech (verb vs. noun) in milliseconds with SE bars

3.3 Morphonotactic vs. Phonotactic

In the comparison of average RTs between the two conditions where the target letters were at the beginning of the word (P1) and the only difference was the boundary type, a facilitation effect was found for the morphonotactic boundary type (compared to the purely phonotactic). Figure 5 shows the average RT and significant difference between the type of boundary (MP or purely phonotactic).

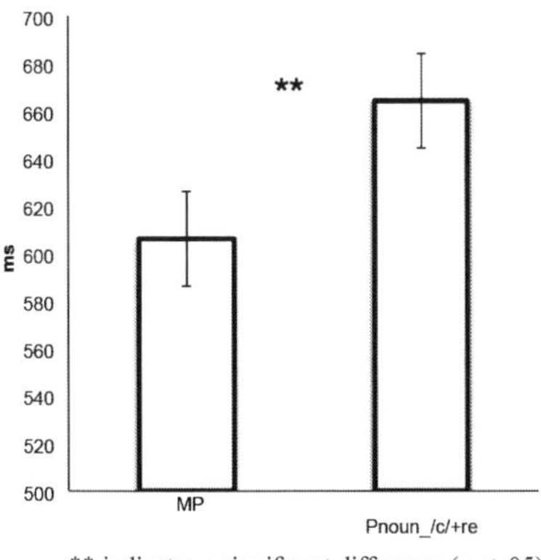

Figure 5. Reaction time results in milliseconds with SE bars of the mean for morphonotactic vs. phonotactic P2 conditions

4. RESULTS 2

It is also interesting to examine the possible correlation between the RT and a set of variables related to all formal (surface) aspects of the words, such as the length in terms of characters, the number of syllables and the orthographic neighbourhood. The reaction times (log) of correct responses were also analysed using a linear mixed-effects model. The fixed factor predictors included are the following:

a) condition (MP verb_RE/P2, P noun_RE/P2, P verb_RE/P1, P noun_RE/P1)

b) ortho_neigh (number of orthographic neighbours)

c) nbsyll (number of syllables),

d) nbletters (number of letters or word length)

e) TP_ORT (orthographic transitions probability)

f) FrWaC_freq (the log frequency of the form in FrWAC corpus, Baroni et al. 2009).

Table 5. Linear mixed-effects results of the reaction time data

Groups	Name	Variance	SD			
Random	effects:					
word	(Intercept)	0.0005587	0.02364			
participant	(Intercept)	0.0317204	0.1781			
Residual	0.0582263	0.2413				
Predictor	Estimate	Std.	Error	df	t	Pr(>|t|)
Fixed effects:	effects:					
(Intercept)	6.263813	0.068259	49.21	91.766	<2e-16	***
Condition P(noun_RE)	0.065327	0.025253	8.35	2.587	0.0312	*
Condition P(RE_noun)	-0.055352	0.031062	13.17	-1.782	0.0978	.
Condition P(RE_verb)	-0.015291	0.038177	18.54	-0.401	0.6933	
ortho_neigh	-0.001171	0.003072	48.53	-0.381	0.7047	
nbsyll	-0.009288	0.022931	50.92	-0.405	0.6871	
nbletters	0.019177	0.010635	49.74	1.803	0.0774	.
TP_ORT	-0.160263	0.180087	46.15	-0.89	0.3781	
log(FrWaC_freq)	-0.00961	0.0038	20.54	-2.529	0.0197	*

Signif. codes: 0 '***' 0.001 '**' 0.01 '*' 0.05 '.' 0.1 ' ' 1

Participants and items were included as random effects. In particular, the TP_ORT variable reports the transitional probability of bigrams corresponding to the last letter of the target word (e.g. <v> in viV-re and the next subsequent letter of the letters to be searched (e.g. viVRe, that is the conditioned probability that an <r> follows a letter <v>). Table 5 shows the results obtained from the linear mixed-effects model and Figure 6 shows the significance of standardized fixed effects.

A significant effect of boundary type is found, showing that participants identify the letters within words that included morphological and phonotactic boundaries faster than in words with a purely phonotactic one (in P2). The intercept (morphonological condition: MP verb_RE/P2, our 'base case') was significant, meaning that the RTs (for finding the letter 'RE' in this condition) seem to reflect a facilitation effect, while the phonological condition (P noun_RE/P2) shows an inhibitory effect (longer RTs are needed to respond). In both of these conditions, the target letters are in the final position of the word (P2).

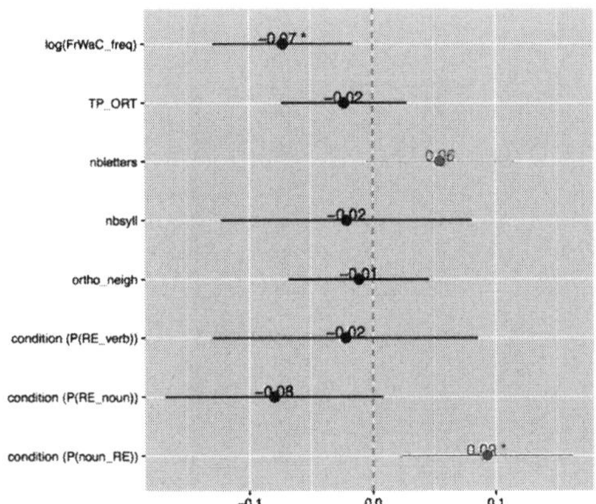

Figure 6. Standardized fixed effects showing that frequency, length and condition are significant

The model predictors are the following (see Figure 7):

a) Condition: Reaction times (log) during the letter search task for each of the boundary-type conditions (1) MP verb_RE/P2, (2) P noun_RE/P2, (3) P verb_RE/P1 and (4) P noun_RE/P1.
b) Frequency (FrWac_freq): The higher the frequency of the word form (same inflectional form), the lower the reaction times responses associated with it.
c) Length (nbletters): Contrary to frequency (and as expected), as the length of the word increases, the RT also increases.

d) Number of Syllables (nbsyll): Follows the trend for the length of the word, but the effect is not significant.
e) Orthographic Neighbours (ortho_neigh): The more orthographic neighbours a word form has, the trend for the reaction times is to decrease, but this is not significant.
f) Transition Probability (TP_ORT): No significant effect was found.

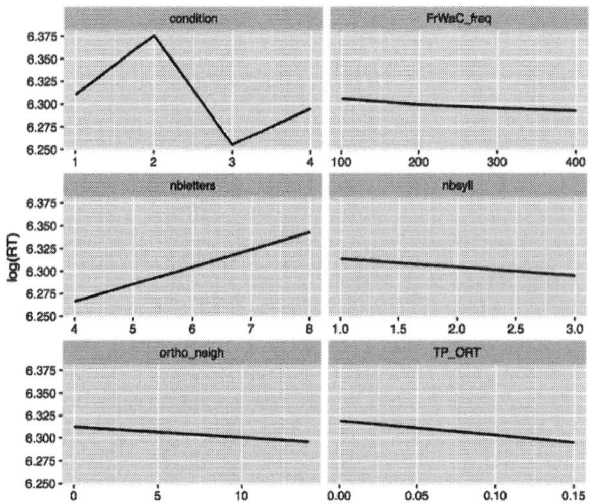

Figure 7. Marginal effects of model predictors

1. CONCLUSION

The Strong Morphonotactic Hypothesis (Dressler & Dziubalska-Kołaczyk 2006) was tested following the letter search task paradigm using words in French with morphonotactic and phonotactic boundaries with different positions for the targets across the materials. The target could be either at the beginning of the word (position 1) or at the end (position 2). Globally, the results showed that prototypical morphonotactic sequences were processed faster than phonotactic sequences, suggesting that phonotactics help us perceive the internal word structure in terms of morphological construction by enhancing their morphological salience. The presented results revealed that this was the case for position 2 (but not position 1): letter search times were longer when the target letters were embedded in a phonotactic condition compared to a morphonotactic one.

Our findings also provide indirect evidence for the left-to-right bias in word-recognition processing asymmetry across word beginnings and ends, and we assume that the mechanisms underlying printed word recognition are shaped by the physical constraints imposed by the reading direction (Giraudo & Grainger 2003). Responses were indeed significantly longer for the items that had the target letters in the second position (P2) compared to those in the first position (P1).

A significant effect of frequency was also obtained, showing that the more frequent a word is, the faster the reaction times are, while all other variables (like orthographic neighbours, transition probability and grammatical category) were found to be not statistically significant. According to our view of morphological processing (Giraudo & Voga 2014; Voga & Giraudo 2017), morphology plays a central role in the cognitive system at two levels: at a perceptive/surface level (when the morphological structure is salient, as is the case for morphonotactic words), and at a central level (where paradigmatic relationships organize the word representations coded in the mental lexicon). We claim that finding sensitivity to morphology and effects of abilities is compatible with a paradigmatic/construction view of morphology (e.g. Booij 2010). On the one hand, morphological salience can speed up lexical access in adult word comprehension and help to develop the morphological awareness of those learning to read. Morphological awareness refers to children's "conscious awareness of the morphemic structure of words and their ability to reflect on and manipulate that structure" (Carlisle 1995: 194). Accordingly, it contributes to reading ability (e.g. Brittain 1970; Carlisle 1995; Deacon & Kirby 2004; Mahony, Singson & Mann 2000; Nagy, Berninger & Abbott 2006; Nunes & Bryant 2006; Kirby et al. 2012). Consequently, morphemes can provide cues for meaning, spelling and pronunciation (e.g. Carlisle 2003). On the other hand, construction representations link morphologically related words at a central level, and the presence or absence of connections is determined by the degree of semantic/functional relationships between the word forms according to their shared morpheme (base or affix). A fundamental assumption of this view is that construction representations are created/emerge and are stabilized in long-term memory according to an ecological rule that imposes family and series clustering as an organizational principle of the mental lexicon. To conclude, the claim is that the mental lexicon is constructed according to multiple dimensions: the perceptive salience of the word's morphological structure (enhanced by morphonotactics) and its formal-semantic relationships with the other coded words, in other words, its syntagmatic and paradigmatic dimensions.

REFERENCES

Baroni, Marco; Bernardini, Silvia; Ferraresi, Adriano & Zanchetta, Eros (2009) The WaCky wide web: A collection of very large linguistically processed web-crawled corpora, *Language Resources and Evaluation* 43(3), 209–226. doi:10.1007/s10579-009-9081-4

Beyersmann, Elisabeth; Casalis, Séverine, Ziegler, Johannes C. & Grainger, Jonathan (2014) Language proficiency and morpho-orthographic segmentation, *Psychonomic bulletin & Review* 22(4), 1054–1061. doi:10.3758/s13423-014-0752-9

Blevins, James P. (2014) The morphology of words. In: Goldrick, Matthew; Ferreira, Victor S. & Miozzo, Michele (eds) *The Oxford Handbook of Language Production*, 152–164. doi:10.1093/oxfordhb/9780199735471.013.018

Booij, Geert (2010) Construction morphology, *Language and Linguistics Compass* 4(7), 543–555. doi:10.1111/j.1749-818X.2010.00213.x

Brittain, Mary M. (1970) Inflectional performance and early reading achievement, *Reading Research Quarterly* 6(1), 34–48. doi:10.2307/747047

Carlisle, Joanne F. (1995) Morphological awareness and early reading achievement. In: Feldman, Laurie B. (ed.) *Morphological Aspects of Language Processing*. Hillsdale, NJ: Erlbaum, 189–209.

Carlisle, Joanne F. (2003) Morphology matters in learning to read: A commentary, *Reading Psychology* 24, 291–332.

Deacon, S. Hélène & Kirby, John R. (2004) Morphological awareness: Just "more phonological"? The roles of morphological and phonological awareness in reading development, *Applied Psycholinguistics* 25(2), 223–238. doi:10.1017.S0124716404001117

Dressler, Wolfgang U. & Dziubalska-Kolaczyk, Katarzyna (2006) Proposing morphonotactis, *Italian Journal of Linguistics* 18(2), 249–266.

Forster, Kenneth I. & Forster, Jonathan C. (2003) DMDX: A Windows display program with millisecond accuracy, *Behavior Research Methods, Instruments & Computers* 35(1), 116–124. doi:10.3758/BF03195503

Giraudo, Hélène & Dal Maso, Serena (2016) The salience of complex words and their parts: Which comes first?, *Frontiers in Psychology* 7, 1778. doi:10.3389/fpsyg.2016.01778

Giraudo, Hélène & Grainger, Jonathan (2003) On the role of derivational affixes in recognizing complex words: Evidence from masked priming. In: Schreuder, Robert & Baayen, R. Harald (eds) *Morphological Structure in Language Processing*. Berlin: De Gruyter Mouton, 209–232. doi:10.1515/9783110910186.209

Giraudo, Hélène & Voga, Madeleine (2014) Measuring morphology: the tip of the iceberg? A retrospective on 10 years of morphological processing, *Cahiers de Grammaire* 22, 136–167.

Kirby, John R.; Deacon, S. Hélene; Bowers, Peter N.; Izenberg, Leah; Wade-Woolley, Lesly; Rauno, Parrila (2012) Children's morphological awareness and reading ability, *Reading and Writing* 25(2), 389–410. doi:10.1007/s11145-010-9276-5

Korecky-Kröll, Katharina; Dressler, Wolfgang U.; Freiberger, Eva M.; Reinisch, Eva; Mörth, Karlheinz & Libben, Gary (2014) Morphonotactic and phonotactic processing in German-speaking adults, *Language Sciences* 46, 48–58. doi:10.1016/j.langsci.2014.06.006

Mahony, Diana; Singson, Maria & Mann, Virginia (2000) Reading ability and sensitivity to morphological relations, *Reading and Writing* 12(3), 191–218. doi:10.1023/A:1008136012492

Nagy, William; Berninger, Virginia W. & Abbott, Robert D. (2006) Contributions of morphology beyond phonology to literacy outcomes of upper elementary and middle-school students, *Journal of Educational Psychology* 98(1), 134–147. doi:10.1037/0022–0663.98.1.134

New, Boris; Pallier, Christophe; Ferrand, Ludovic & Matos, Rafael (2001) Une base de données lexicales du français contemporain sur internet: LEXIQUE™ (A lexical database for contemporary French: LEXIQUE™), *L'année Psychologique* 101(3), 447–462. doi:10.3406/psy.2001.1341

Nunes, Terezinha & Bryant, Peter (eds) (2006) *Improving Literacy by Teaching Morphemes*. London: Routledge.

Taft, Marcus & Forster, Kenneth I. (1975) Lexical storage and retrieval of prefixed words. *Journal of Verbal Learning and Verbal Behavior* 14(6), 638–647.

Voga, Madeleine & Giraudo, Hélène (2017) Word and beyond word issues in morphological processing, *Word Structure* 10(2), 235–255. doi:10.3366/word.2017.0109

Subject Index

A

accuracy 66, 78, 80–82, 88–89, 91–95, 97, 103, 105, 128

acoustic/s, acoustically 10, 12, 55–56, 59, 61–62, 66, 72–73

acquisition

- first language 16, 43, 55, 73, 77, 79–80, 97, 102, 123
- of morphology 78
- of morphonotactic clusters 77, 79–80, 104–105
- of phonotactic clusters 79–80, 104

acquisitional 7, 13, 78, 103–105

adolescent/adult language processing 80–82, 92, 97, 102

affix/ation 16, 20, 42, 88, 124, 135

B

Beats-and-Binding model 15, 18, 102, 104

phonological boundary/ies 12, 125–126

phonotactic boundary/ies 126, 130, 133–134

C

casual speech; *see also* speech production 15, 44

chunking 97, 124

cluster/s

- quadruple 16, 22–27, 31, 44, 47
- triple 9, 15–16, 19, 21–22, 26–27, 29–31, 33–41, 43, 45–47

complex/ity 12, 15, 17, 22–23, 38, 41, 43–44, 47, 77–78, 103, 105–108, 123–125

compound/s, compounding 10–11, 16, 20, 26, 29–30, 41–43, 55, 77–78, 83–87, 89–94, 96–97

consonantal language 15, 19, 46

corpus linguistic 7, 9, 16, 20–21, 41, 78

D

decomposition 20, 89, 123–124

default 17, 19, 23–24, 26, 28–29, 81

deletion/s 8, 16, 42, 44–46, 54–55, 59, 62, 65–66, 78

derivation/s, derivational 10–11, 16, 20, 27–28, 30, 37–38, 41–42, 44–46, 78, 83, 85–87, 89–94, 96–97

derivative 77, 96–97, 125

development/al 11–12, 44, 46, 79, 105, 107, 110, 112–113, 115, 117

diachronic, diachrony 21, 24, 43–46

E

elicitation task 103

English 7–8, 15–17, 23, 28–29, 34–35, 45–46, 54–55, 80, 93, 102–105, 115–116

epenthesis 11, 108

experiment/s, experimental 7, 9–10, 12, 28, 43, 77, 80–91, 93–97, 85, 123–125, 127

F

facilitate, facilitation 11–12, 16, 20, 55, 58, 77–78, 81–82, 88–89, 94, 97, 104, 117, 125, 129–131, 133

familiarity

- effect/s 11, 77, 92, 95–97
- rating/s 84, 90–91, 95

foreignness

- effect/s 77, 92, 95–96
- rating/s 84, 87–88, 90–91

fragment monitoring task 82

French 9–12, 56–57, 60, 67–68, 71, 101, 103, 105–109, 112, 115–117, 124–127, 134

frequency effect/s 11, 77, 92, 94–97

G

German 7–12, 15–16, 19–22, 26, 29, 34, 38–39, 42–47, 53–54, 56–57, 66, 71, 73–74, 77–86, 88–92, 95–98, 101, 104–106, 115, 123

Germanic 8, 12, 15, 23, 42, 45–46

H
homophones 55, 66, 71
homophonous 28, 35, 37, 53–57, 61, 77–78, 104

I
inflection/al 8, 11, 20–21, 37, 42, 44–46, 78, 83, 86–89, 97, 103, 105, 126, 133

L
language awareness 82
latency; *see also* reaction times 77, 82, 88–89, 95–96
lexical
access 78, 82, 84, 123–125, 135
diversity 25
level 82
lexical decision task 10, 83–84, 87–90
Lithuanian 11, 43, 73, 78, 80, 104–105

M
marked/ness 7, 9, 18, 22, 33, 43, 47, 53, 101–102, 104–105
mix/ed sounds 11
monomorphemic word/s 17, 66, 83–87, 89–93, 97
morpheme boundary/ies 10, 16–17, 20, 29, 41–42, 44, 53–56, 58, 66, 68–74, 77, 79–83, 85, 88–90, 92–97, 101, 123
morphological awareness 135
morphological boundary/ies 12, 105, 116, 123, 125, 133
morphological processing 12, 125, 135
morphological richness 10, 73, 78–80, 89
morphonology 18, 82
morphonotactic boundary/ies 12, 125, 131, 134
morphonotactic cluster/s 8, 10, 20–22, 28, 37, 41, 45, 53–56, 66, 73–74, 78–80, 82, 85, 90, 92–93, 94, 96
morphotactic 7–8, 16, 20, 29, 77, 104–105, 109, 126

N
NAD 9, 18–20, 22, 24, 30–34, 36, 38, 40–41, 44–45, 105
Natural Morphology 15, 20
Natural Phonology 15, 18
Net Auditory Distance model; *see* NAD

O
omission 11, 108–109, 113–115, 117
opacity, opaque 20, 24, 28–29, 44

P
part of speech 21, 126, 129–131
peripheral cluster/s, position 22, 34, 41, 43, 45–46
phonetic realization 10, 53–54, 66, 74, 108
phonotactic cluster/s 10, 28, 41, 45, 53–57, 73–74, 77, 79–80, 82, 85, 90, 92–93
Polish 11, 15, 34, 43, 45–46, 73, 78, 80, 88, 101, 104–105
preferred/ness 7, 9, 16, 18–20, 31–38, 40–41, 45–46
processing cost/s 78, 83, 88, 117
productivity 18, 21, 26, 97
progressive demasking task 10, 83–84, 86
pronunciation 11, 24, 44, 101, 108, 110–112, 115, 135

R
reaction times; *see also* latency 81, 84, 88, 95–96, 123, 128, 131–135
reduction/s 10–11, 27, 54, 56, 58, 72–73, 108, 113–115
repetition 11, 108

S
salience, salient 12, 20, 125, 130, 134–135
shift/ed cluster 11, 108
simplex word/s 17, 77, 83, 88–89, 92–96
Slavic 8–9, 15, 23, 43–47, 78
Slovak 15, 44–46
speech production; *see also* casual speech 9–10, 12, 53–56, 66, 72–74, 103
split cluster task 81, 96
Strong Morphonotactic Hypothesis 8–10, 12, 16, 56, 78, 80, 88–89, 97, 101, 104–106, 116–117, 123, 134
sublexical level 81–82, 88, 96, 124
substitution 11, 108, 113–114
syllable/s 7, 16–18, 41, 43, 45, 59, 68–69, 86, 97, 102–103, 108, 111, 116, 132, 134

syllable boundary/ies 41–42

T

token frequency 9, 18, 22, 24, 26, 28–29, 41, 44–45, 92–95
transparency, transparent 20, 24, 83, 124
type frequency 9, 18, 25–26, 28–29, 41, 45
type-token ratio 24–26, 47
typological 9, 15–16, 20, 44, 53

U

unstressed position 15, 45

V

visual word recognition task 78, 82, 87, 124

W

word boundary/ies 17, 55, 102
word-final cluster/s 23, 26, 30, 34–35, 41, 46, 61, 73, 79, 103, 105, 113, 116–117
word-final position/s 9, 11–12, 15, 19, 23, 34, 45–46, 57, 62, 79–82, 102–103, 109, 112–113, 116, 125–126, 129, 133
word-initial cluster/s 9, 20–23, 35, 38–41, 44, 46, 79, 102–103, 105, 109, 112, 116–117, 126
word-initial position/s 11–12, 15, 19, 21, 34, 38, 41, 44–46, 57, 79, 81, 102–103, 108–109, 111–112, 123, 125–126, 129
word-internal boundary/ies 10, 42, 53, 55–56
word-internal cluster/s 20–21, 41–42, 45
word-internal/ly position 41
word-medial cluster/s 10, 19, 41, 46, 53, 57, 59, 67, 69–72, 103, 105
word-medial position/s 11, 19, 44, 57, 59–60, 67, 71, 79–82, 85, 108–110, 112–113, 116, 123